Walt Whitman

Out of the Cradle
Endlessly Rocking

Edited by
Dominick P. Consolo
Denison University

The Merrill Literary
Casebook Series
Edward P. J. Corbett, Editor

Charles E. Merrill Publishing Company
A Bell & Howell Company
Columbus, Ohio

236671

ISBN: 0-675-09254-X

Library of Congress Catalog Number: 70-138465

1 2 3 4 5 6 7 8 9 10—75 74 73 72 71

PS
3222
09
1971

Printed in the United States of America

Foreword

The Charles E. Merrill Literary Casebook Series deals with short literary works, arbitrarily defined here as "works which can be easily read in a single sitting." Accordingly, the series will concentrate on poems, short stories, brief dramas, and literary essays. These casebooks are designed to be used in literature courses or in practical criticism courses where the instructor wants to expose his students to an extensive and intensive study of a single, short work or in composition courses where the instructor wants to expose his students to the discipline of writing a research paper on a literary text.

All of the casebooks in the series follow this format: (1) foreword; (2) the author's introduction; (3) the text of the literary work; (4) a number of critical articles on the literary work; (5) suggested topics for short papers on the literary work; (6) suggested topics for long (10-15 pages) papers on the literary work; (7) a selective bibliography of additional readings on the literary work; (8) general instructions for the writing of a research paper. Some of the casebooks, especially those dealing with poetry, may carry an additional section, which contains such features as variant versions of the work, a closely related literary work, comments by the author and his contemporaries on the work.

So that students might simulate first-hand research in library copies of books and bound periodicals, each of the critical articles carries full bibliographical information at the bottom of the first page of the article, and the text of the article carries the actual page-numbers of the original source. A notation like /131/ after a word in the text indicates that *after* that word in the original source the article went over to page 131. All of the text between that number and the next number, /132/, can be taken as occurring on page 131 of the original source.

Edward P.J. Corbett
General Editor

Contents

Contributors

DOMINICK CONSOLO, the editor, is a professor of English at Denison University. A Fulbright Lecturer at Tel-Aviv University in Israel (1964-65), he has written studies of Graham Greene, articles on American writers for World Book Encyclopedia, edited D. H. Lawrence's "The Rocking-Horse Winner," a Merrill literary casebook, and co-edited a contemporary anthology, *Black Drama*. He is writing a full-length study of contemporary fiction.

GAY WILSON ALLEN, professor of English at New York University, is the author of numerous books including *Walt Whitman Handbook* and a critical biography, *The Solitary Singer*.

ROY P. BASLER, Chief of the Reference Department Manuscript Division at the Library of Congress, is the author of *Sex, Symbolism, and Psychology in Literature*.

HENRY S. CANBY, one of the editors of *A Literary History of the United States*, has written *Walt Whitman, an American* and numerous other studies.

RICHARD CHASE has written many books on American writers including *The American Novel and Its Tradition* and *Walt Whitman Reconsidered*.

CHARLES T. DAVIS, a professor of English at Pennsylvania State University, is author of *Edwin Arlington Robinson: Selected Early Poems and Letters*.

ROBERT D. FANER was a professor and Chairman of English at Southern Illinois University, Carbondale.

CLARK GRIFFITH has published many articles on American writers and a study of Emily Dickinson's tragic poetry, *The Long Shadow*. He is a professor of English at the University of Oregon.

EMORY HOLLOWAY, emeritus professor of English, Queens College, has written extensively on Whitman and edited, among other works, *The Uncollected Poetry and Prose*.

NEIL D. ISAACS, associate professor of English at the University of Tennessee, edited *Tolkien and the Critics*.

EDWIN H. MILLER, chairman of the department of English, University College, New York University, is editor of *The Correspondence of Walt Whitman* (5 vols.).

JAMES E. MILLER, a professor of English at the University of Chicago, has published several studies of American writers, including *Reader's Guide to Herman Melville*.

ROY HARVEY PEARCE is a professor of American Literature at the University of California, San Diego. In addition to many articles on American writers and Intellectual History, he has published *The Continuity of American Poetry*.

LEO SPITZER, distinguished scholar and professor, made lasting contributions to the fields of linguistics, literary history, and comparative literature.

FLOYD STOVALL, former Poe Professor at the University of Virginia, is editor of *Walt Whitman's Prose Works* (2 vols.).

CHARLES C. WALCUTT is the author of numerous articles and books, including *Man's Changing Mask*. He is a professor of English at Queens College.

STEPHEN E. WHICHER was an associate professor of English at Cornell University and edited *Selections from Ralph Waldo Emerson*.

Introduction

It goes without saying that " Out of the Cradle Endlessly Rocking"
is one of Whitman's finest poems. And yet, when the poem was published in the New York *Saturday Press* (December 24, 1859), under its
first title, "A Child's Reminiscence," it was attacked with high glee in
a slashing article in the *Cincinnati Daily Commercial*.[1] The poet (with
transparent anonymity) wrote an apologia in reply that began with the
following statement:

> What is the reason-why of Walt Whitman's lyric utterances, as soon
> as any of them is heard, rousing up such vehement intellectual censures
> and contumely from some persons, and then equally determined bravos
> from other persons?[2]

It was a just appraisal of his readers, valid for the time and prophetic
as well. Abuse or adulation, ridicule or praise—these were the characteristic attitudes, and they were already familiar ones to Whitman.

Emerson had provided the "bravos." In a congratulatory letter to
the poet upon receiving a personal copy of the first edition of *Leaves
of Grass* (1855), Emerson defined the slim volume as the "most extraordinary piece of wit and wisdom that America has yet contrib-
uted," discovering in it "incomparable things said incomparably well."
A critic for the *New York Times*, on the other hand, gave public evidence of the "censures and contumely" that were to plague Whitman.
His strident review attacked both the man and the poetry. "What
centaur have we here, half man, half beast, neighing defiance to the
world . . . who proclaims himself the poet of his time, and who roots
like a pig among the rotten garbage of licentious thoughts?" In the
face of such ignorant abuse, one can understand why more than

---

[1] See the complete article, "Walt Whitman's New Poem," in this volume.
[2] Whitman's reply, "All About a Mocking-Bird" is also printed here and follows
the above.

1

bruised ego led him to anonymous defenses of his poetry and to patient explanations of intention.

Designedly, he prefaced the first appearance of "Out of the Cradle" with explanatory comments. Calling the poem a "wild and plaintive song, well-enveloped," Whitman described its effect as being that of music and eluding definition. This was not to say, however, what the Cincinnati critic seized upon, that the poem was without meaning. As the variety of interpretations in this collection reveals, the poem is replete with meanings. The elusiveness of which Whitman spoke is what escapes definition in all great poetry. And it is on the point of the poem's greatness that the following essays, but one, agree. For that exception, time has nicely proved the narrowness of that critic's judgment.

What Whitman had chanted in another context, ("I am large, I contain multitudes"), may be true in a sense of this collection of essays. Though all of them have been written in the present century, none of the writers need fear the judgment of time. None does violence to the poem, although their approaches to the poem vary according to their particular concerns. Some approaches combine explication with biographical considerations, attempting to discover through both poem and the poet's personal life what lay behind an apparent emotional crisis. Was it the result of a failed love affair? And if so, was the lover female or male? Can one account for the dark emphasis on the theme of separation and loss, on death as an end, rather than an "accouchement"? What stilled the "barbaric yawp" of a few years earlier and replaced it with a lyrical cry of felt anguish? These questions are brilliantly explored in separate essays by Stephen E. Whicher and Clark Griffith, and each author provides answers of his own. Emory Holloway finds the suffering of personal loss in the poem's imagery. Edwin H. Miller explores the poem as an "inner drama," a "psychological journey" of intuitive insights put into artistic order by the poet's genius.

The approaches to the poem through form or genre demonstrate convincingly that Whitman was a great artist and that his poems can be read with the same close attention to imagery and detail one gives to more obviously structured verse. Robert D. Faner draws fine parallels between "Out of the Cradle" and Italian opera; Richard Chase treats it as a "romance." Leo Spitzer, seeing the poem in the context of world literature, combines astonishing scholarship and poetic sensibility in his explication of the poem as an "ode." Roy Harvey Pearce, using the 1860 version, "A Word Out of the Sea," as his text, argues persuasively for the conscious artistry of Whitman, placing the emphasis on the very act of creation.[3] James E. Miller provides a sensitive reading in a close analysis of the poem's final version. There are some views held in common by the writers in this volume, but the differences are equally marked. In all instances their prose speaks of their sincere engagement, an involvement inspired by the poem to get at its meaning.

Poetry begins with feeling that finds its expression in words. The source of that feeling may lie in immediate or past experience, either real or fancied, and can never be known with absolute certainty. Thus where it is not narrowly biographical, interest in what has occasioned a poem involves one ultimately in a concern with the creative process.

Yet "Out of the Cradle," as does most of Whitman's poetry, tempts the reader away from the creative act toward the biographical, to search out something of the poet's personal life. For no other poet of equal stature, certainly no American poet, made such deliberate attempts to become part and parcel of his own creations. The poet created the roles, and the living man assumed them. Walter became Walt, the cravat gave way to the open collar, the dilettante became one of the roughs, the editor advanced to the god-head. Finally, in the figure of the good grey poet, Whitman became the father to all. The particulars behind the masks and in the poems speak of darker things, and of these, critical biographers such as Roger Asselineau and Gay Wilson Allen have much to say. But one can become so preoccupied with the discrepancies between the man and his masks as to lose sight of the poetry, which, in the final analysis, is what matters.

A principal attraction of Whitman's poetry, it seems to me, is that of its single subject—the creative process. Greatly diverse though his poems may be in theme and mood, the genuine subject of each is always one and the same. Each celebrates the miraculous nature of language and the creative process that discovers it and orders it into poetry. The poems are journeys into an uncharted region where meaning must await the poet's own discovery of it through the poem. Since the process is an organic one, allowing imaginative experience to shape its own form, free verse is natural to it. A single unit of meaning determines the length of the line. Each line, in turn, becomes one in a series of momentary illuminations that formalize into the poem. If this is true for the poet, it is no less true for the reader. Using the poem as his guide, he recreates the process whereby the poet discovered his meaning. As it were, he shares in that discovery at the

---

[3] This is fully developed in his introduction to the 1860 facsimile edition of *Leaves of Grass.* See Bibliography.

very moment the poet orders it into words. Thus, the creative process itself is the subject matter of the poem, whatever its theme.

Whitman suggested as much in responding to the criticism of his first version of "Out of the Cradle," where he was charged with obscurity of meaning. What the mocking-bird means, what it infers, he said, can only be interpreted "out of the soul. Pursue the chants awhile, listen—yield yourself—persevere."

This book presents those "chants" in two complete versions, that of 1860 and the final version of 1891–92. The poems are printed on facing pages to allow for an uninterrupted reading of each. For the purposes of criticism, critical or textual, this format permits a systematic comparison of the two versions, line by line. The changes are few in number, as the spatial arrangement readily shows, yet they are significant enough, as some of the critics included here contend, to effect a different reading for each poem. Whitman made most of the changes for the 1867 edition of *Leaves of Grass*. The title by which the poem has become familiar, "Out of the Cradle Endlessly Rocking," was not used until 1871, heading a cluster of poems called "Sea-Shore Memories" in the *Passage to India* edition. The final substantive change, though, occurred in 1881, when Whitman added the controversial penultimate line to the poem: "(Or like some old crone rocking the cradle, swathed in sweet garments, bending aside)."

Differences between the first version (1859) and that of the following year are slight but significant in any study of organic form. Whitman titled the poem "A Child's Reminiscence," and printed below it the term PRE–VERSE, in capital letters. The title is a rhetorical guide to the poem and the focus of our attention is on the child and the past action, the reminiscence. The opening section concluded with the following lines:

> Throwing myself on the sand, I
> Confronting the waves, sing.

The 1860 version, however, shows the addition of two lines that shift the emphasis to the narrator and the present action.

> Throwing myself on the sand, confronting the waves,
> I, chanter of pains and joys, uniter of here and hereafter,
> Taking all hints to use them—but swiftly leaping beyond them,
> A reminiscence sing.

Since these additional lines define the "I" and in effect, modify the first title's directive, Whitman needed a title to reinforce the change, or at best to balance his new perspective on the poem. He chose, "A Word Out of the Sea," a title that points backward to the reminiscence but also incorporates the present action. What was Whitman "yielding" himself to when he responded to the poem, and why?

It was perhaps wise of Whitman to abandon altogether the attempt to define the poem through its title and to let it be known, in the final version, by its opening line. In any event, he had accurately named the poem when it first sang to him. In his prefatory note giving the poem to the world, he began:

> Our readers may, if they choose, consider as our Christmas or New Year's present to them, the curious warble, by Walt Whitman. . . .

A Word Out of the Sea

(Reprinted from the 1860 edition of *Leaves of Grass*.)

Out of the rocked cradle,
Out of the mocking-bird's throat, the musical shuttle,
Out of the boy's mother's womb, and from the nipples of
    her breasts,
Out of the Ninth Month midnight,
Over the sterile sands, and the fields beyond, where the
    child, leaving his bed, wandered alone, bareheaded,
    barefoot,
Down from the showered halo,
Up from the mystic play of shadows, twining and twisting
    as if they were alive,
Out from the patches of briers and blackberries,
From the memories of the bird that chanted to me,
From your memories, sad brother—from the fitful risings
    and fallings I heard,
From under that yellow half-moon, late-risen, and swollen
    as if with tears,
From those beginning notes of sickness and love, there in
    the transparent mist,
From the thousand responses of my heart, never to cease,
From the myriad thence-aroused words,
From the word stronger and more delicious than any,
From such, as now they start, the scene revisiting,
As a flock, twittering, rising, or overhead passing,
Borne hither—ere all eludes me, hurriedly,
A man—yet by these tears a little boy again,
Throwing myself on the sand, confronting the waves,
I, chanter of pains and joys, uniter of here and hereafter,
Taking all hints to use them—but swiftly leaping beyond
    them,
A reminiscence sing.

REMINISCENCE

1. Once, Paumanok,
    When the snows had melted, and the Fifth Month
    grass was growing,

each poem is a journey

Out of the Cradle Endlessly Rocking

(Final revised version 1881)

Out of the cradle endlessly rocking,
Out of the mocking-bird's throat, the musical shuttle,
Out of the Ninth-month midnight,
Over the sterile sands and the fields beyond, where the
    child leaving his bed wander'd alone, bareheaded,
    barefoot,
Down from the shower'd halo,   5
Up from the mystic play of shadows twining and twisting
    as if they were alive,
Out from the patches of briers and blackberries,
From the memories of the bird that chanted to me,
From your memories sad brother, from the fitful risings
    and fallings I heard,
From under that yellow half-moon late-risen and swollen
    as if with tears,   10
From those beginning notes of yearning and love there in
    the mist,
From the thousand responses of my heart never to cease,
From the myriad thence-arous'd words,
From the word stronger and more delicious than any,
From such as now they start the scene revisiting,   15
As a flock, twittering, rising, or overhead passing,
Borne hither, ere all eludes me, hurriedly,
A man, yet by these tears a little boy again,
Throwing myself on the sand, confronting the waves,
I, chanter of pains and joys, uniter of here and hereafter,   20
Taking all hints to use them, but swiftly leaping beyond
    them,
A reminiscence sing.

Once Paumanok,
When the lilac-scent was in the air and Fifth-month grass
    was growing,

Up this sea-shore, in some briers,
Two guests from Alabama—two together,
And their nest, and four light-green eggs, spotted with
    brown,
And every day the he-bird, to and fro, near at hand,
And every day the she-bird, crouched on her nest,
    silent, with bright eyes,
And every day I, a curious boy, never too close, never
    disturbing them,
Cautiously peering, absorbing, translating.

2. *Shine! Shine!*
  Pour down your warmth, great Sun!
  While we bask—we two together.

3. *Two together!*
  Winds blow South, or winds blow North,
  Day come white, or night come black,
  Home, or rivers and mountains from home,
  Singing all time, minding no time,
  If we two but keep together.

4. Till of a sudden,
  May-be killed, unknown to her mate,
  One forenoon the she-bird crouched not on the nest,
  Nor returned that afternoon, nor the next,
  Nor ever appeared again.

5. And thenceforward, all summer, in the sound of the
    sea,
  And at night, under the full of the moon, in calmer
    weather,
  Over the hoarse surging of the sea,
  Or flitting from brier to brier by day,
  I saw, I heard at intervals, the remaining one, the he-
    bird,
  The solitary guest from Alabama.

6. *Blow! Blow!*
  Blow up sea-winds along Paumanok's shore;
  I wait and I wait, till you blow my mate to me.

7. Yes, when the stars glistened,
  All night long, on the prong of a moss-scallop'd stake,
  Down, almost amid the slapping waves,
  Sat the lone singer, wonderful, causing tears.

Up this seashore in some briers,   25
Two feather'd guests from Alabama, two together,
And their nest, and four light-green eggs spotted with
    brown,
And every day the he-bird to and fro near at hand,
And every day the she-bird crouch'd on her nest, silent,
    with bright eyes,
And every day I, a curious boy, never too close, never
    disturbing them,   30
Cautiously peering, absorbing, translating.

Shine! shine! shine!
Pour down your warmth, great sun!
While we bask, we two together.

Two together!   35
Winds blow south, or winds blow north,
Day come white, or night come black,
Home, or rivers and mountains from home,
Singing all time, minding no time,
While we two keep together.   40

Till of a sudden,
May-be kill'd, unknown to her mate,
One forenoon the she-bird crouch'd not on the nest,
Nor return'd that afternoon, nor the next,
Nor ever appear'd again.   45

And thenceforward all summer in the sound of the sea,
And at night under the full of the moon in calmer weather,
Over the hoarse surging of the sea,
Or flitting from brier to brier by day,
I saw, I heard at intervals the remaining one, the he-bird,   50
The solitary guest from Alabama.

Blow! blow! blow!
Blow up sea-winds along Paumanok's shore;
I wait and I wait till you blow my mate to me.

Yes, when the stars glisten'd,   55
All night long on the prong of a moss-scallop'd stake,
Down almost amid the slipping waves,
Sat the lone singer wonderful causing tears.

8. He called on his mate,
   He poured forth the meanings which I, of all men,
       know.

9. Yes, my brother, I know,
   The rest might not—but I have treasured every note,
   For once, and more than once, dimly, down to the
       beach gliding,
   Silent, avoiding the moonbeams, blending myself with
       the shadows,
   Recalling now the obscure shapes, the echoes, the
       sounds and sights after their sorts.
   The white arms out in the breakers tirelessly tossing,
   I, with bare feet, a child, the wind wafting my hair,
   Listened long and long.

10. Listened, to keep, to sing—now translating the notes,
    Following you, my brother.

11. *Soothe! Soothe!*
    Close on its wave soothes the wave behind,
    And again another behind, embracing and lapping,
        every one close,
    But my love soothes not me.

12. *Low hangs the moon—it rose late,*
    O it is lagging—O I think it is heavy with love.

13. *O madly the sea pushes upon the land,*
    With love—with love.

14. *O night!*
    O do I not see my love fluttering out here among the
        breakers?
    What is that little thing I see there in the white?

15. *Loud! Loud!*
    Loud I call to you my love!
    High and clear I shoot my voice over the waves,
    Surely you must know who is here,
    You must know who I am, my love.

16. *Low-hanging moon!*
    What is that dusky spot in your brown yellow?
    O it is the shape of my mate!
    O moon, do not keep her from me any longer.

He call'd on his mate,
He pour'd forth the meanings which I of all men know.   60

Yes my brother I know,
The rest might not, but I have treasur'd every note,
For more than once dimly down to the beach gliding,
Silent, avoiding the moonbeams, blending myself with the
    shadows,
Recalling now the obscure shapes, the echoes, the sounds
    and sights after their sorts,   65
The white arms out in the breakers tirelessly tossing,
I, with bare feet, a child, the wind wafting my hair,
Listen'd long and long.

Listen'd to keep, to sing, now translating the notes,
Following you my brother.   70

Soothe! soothe! soothe!
Close on its wave soothes the wave behind,
And again another behind embracing and lapping, every
    one close,
But my love soothes not me, not me.

Low hangs the moon, it rose late,   75
It is lagging—O I think it is heavy with love, with love.

O madly the sea pushes upon the land,
With love, with love.

O night! do I not see my love fluttering out among the
    breakers?
What is that little black thing I see there in the white?   80

Loud! loud! loud!
Loud I call to you, my love!

High and clear I shoot my voice over the waves,
Surely you must know who is here, is here,
You must know who I am, my love.   85

Low-hanging moon!
What is that dusky spot in your brown yellow?
O it is the shape, the shape of my mate!
O moon do not keep her from me any longer.

17. *Land! O land!*
    Whichever way I turn, O I think you could give me
    *   my mate back again, if you would,*
    For I am almost sure I see her dimly whichever way
    *   I look.*

18. *O rising stars!*
    Perhaps the one I want so much will rise with some of
    *   you.*

19. *O throat!*
    Sound clearer through the atmosphere!
    Pierce the woods, the earth,
    Somewhere listening to catch you must be the one I
    *   want.*

20. *Shake out, carols!*
    Solitary here—the night's carols!
    Carols of lonesome love! Death's carols!
    Carols under that lagging, yellow, waning moon!
    O, under that moon, where she droops almost down
    *   into the sea!*
    O reckless, despairing carols.

21. *But soft!*
    Sink low—soft!
    Soft! Let me just murmur,
    And do you wait a moment, you husky-noised sea,
    For somewhere I believe I heard my mate responding
    *   to me,*
    So faint—I must be still to listen,
    But not altogether still, for then she might not come
    *   immediately to me.*

22. *Hither, my love!*
    Here I am! Here!
    With this just-sustained note I announce myself to you,
    This gentle call is for you, my love.

23. *Do not be decoyed elsewhere!*
    That is the whistle of the wind—it is not my voice,
    That is the fluttering of the spray,
    Those are the shadows of leaves.

24. *O darkness! O in vain!*
    O I am very sick and sorrowful.

Land! land! O land! 90
Whichever way I turn, O I think you could give me my
    mate back again if you only would,
For I am almost sure I see her dimly whichever way I look.

O rising stars!
Perhaps the one I want so much will rise, will rise with
    some of you.

O throat! O trembling throat! 95
Sound clearer through the atmosphere!
Pierce the woods, the earth,
Somewhere listening to catch you must be the one I want.

Shake out carols!
Solitary here, the night's carols! 100
Carols of lonesome love! death's carols!
Carols under that lagging, yellow, waning moon!
O under that moon where she droops almost down into the
    sea!
O reckless despairing carols.

But soft! sink low! 105
Soft! let me just murmur,
And do you wait a moment you husky-nois'd sea,
For somewhere I believe I heard my mate responding
    to me,
So faint, I must be still, be still to listen,
But not altogether still, for then she might not come im-
    mediately to me. 110

Hither my love!
Here I am! here!
With this just-sustain'd note I announce myself to you,
This gentle call is for you my love, for you.

Do not be decoy'd elsewhere, 115
That is the whistle of the wind, it is not my voice,
That is the fluttering, the fluttering of the spray,
Those are the shadows of leaves.

O darkness! O in vain!
O I am very sick and sorrowful. 120

25. *O brown halo in the sky, near the moon, drooping*
    upon the sea!
    O troubled reflection in the sea!
    O throat! O throbbing heart!
    O all—and I singing uselessly all the night.

26. *Murmur! Murmur on!*
    O murmurs—you yourselves make me continue to
    sing, I know not why.

27. *O past! O joy!*
    In the air—in the woods—over fields,
    Loved! Loved! Loved! Loved! Loved!
    Loved—but no more with me,
    We two together no more.

28. The aria sinking,
    All else continuing—the stars shining,
    The winds blowing—the notes of the wondrous bird
        echoing,
    With angry moans the fierce old mother yet, as ever,
        incessantly moaning,
    On the sands of Paumanok's shore gray and rustling,
    The yellow half-moon, enlarged, sagging down, droop-
        ing, the face of the sea almost touching,
    The boy extatic—with his bare feet the waves, with
        his hair the atmosphere dallying,
    The love in the heart pent, now loose, now at last
        tumultuously bursting,
    The aria's meaning, the ears, the Soul, swiftly
        depositing,
    The strange tears down the cheeks coursing,
    The colloquy there—the trio—each uttering,
    The undertone—the savage old mother, incessantly
        crying,
    To the boy's Soul's questions sullenly timing—some
        drowned secret hissing,
    To the outsetting bard of love.

29. Bird! (then said the boy's Soul,)
    Is it indeed toward your mate you sing? or is it mostly
        to me?
    For I that was a child, my tongue's use sleeping,
    Now that I have heard you,

*O brown halo in the sky near the moon, drooping upon
    the sea!*
O troubled reflection in the sea!
O throat! O throbbing heart!
And I singing uselessly, uselessly all the night.

O past! O happy life! O songs of joy!   125
In the air, in the woods, over fields,
Loved! loved! loved! loved! loved!
But my mate no more, no more with me!
We two together no more.

The aria sinking,   130
All else continuing, the stars shining,
The winds blowing, the notes of the bird continuous
    echoing,
With angry moans the fierce old mother incessantly moan-
    ing,
On the sands of Paumanok's shore gray and rustling,
The yellow half-moon enlarged, sagging down, drooping,
    the face of the sea almost touching,   135
The boy ecstatic, with his bare feet the waves, with his
    hair the atmosphere dallying,
The love in the heart long pent, now loose, now at last
    tumultuously bursting,
The aria's meaning, the ears, the soul, swiftly depositing,
The strange tears down the cheeks coursing,
The colloquy there, the trio, each uttering,   140
The undertone, the savage old mother incessantly crying,
To the boy's soul's questions sullenly timing, some drown'd
    secret hissing,
To the outsetting bard.

Demon or bird! (said the boy's soul,)
Is it indeed toward your mate you sing? or is it really to
    me?   145
For I, that was a child, my tongue's use sleeping, now I
    have heard you,

Now in a moment I know what I am for—I awake,
And already a thousand singers—a thousand songs,
    clearer, louder, more sorrowful than yours,
A thousand warbling echoes have started to life within
    me,
Never to die.

30. O throes!
    O you demon, singing by yourself—projecting me,
    O solitary me, listening—never more shall I cease
        imitating, perpetuating you,
    Never more shall I escape,
    Never more shall the reverberations,
    Never more the cries of unsatisfied love be absent
        from me,
    Never again leave me to be the peaceful child I was
        before what there, in the night,
    By the sea, under the yellow and sagging moon,
    The dusky demon aroused—the fire, the sweet hell
        within,
    The unknown want, the destiny of me.

31. O give me some clew!
    O if I am to have so much, let me have more!
    O a word! O what is my destination?
    O I fear it is henceforth chaos!
    O how joys, dreads, convolutions, human shapes, and
        all shapes, spring as from graves around me!
    O phantoms! you cover all the land, and all the sea!
    O I cannot see in the dimness whether you smile or
        frown upon me;
    O vapor, a look, a word! O well-beloved!
    O you dear women's and men's phantoms!

32. A word then, (for I will conquer it,)
    The word final, superior to all,
    Subtle, sent up—what is it?—I listen;
    Are you whispering it, and have been all the time, you
        sea-waves?
    Is that it from your liquid rims and wet sands?

Now in a moment I know what I am for, I awake,
And already a thousand singers, a thousand songs, clearer,
     louder and more sorrowful than yours,
A thousand warbling echoes have started to life within
     me, never to die.
O you singer solitary, singing by yourself, projecting me,   150
O solitary me listening, never more shall I cease perpetu-
     ating you,
Never more shall I escape, never more the reverberations,
Never more the cries of unsatisfied love be absent from me,
Never again leave me to be the peaceful child I was before
     what there in the night,
By the sea under the yellow and sagging moon,   155
The messenger there arous'd, the fire, the sweet hell within,
The unknown want, the destiny of me.

O give me the clew! (it lurks in the night here some-
     where,)
O if I am to have so much, let me have more!

A word then, (for I will conquer it,)   160
The word final, superior to all,
Subtle, sent up—what is it?—I listen;
Are you whispering it, and have been all the time, you
     sea-waves?
Is that it from your liquid rims and wet sands?

33. Answering, the sea,
    Delaying not, hurrying not,
    Whispered me through the night, and very plainly
        before daybreak,
    Lisped to me constantly the low and delicious word
        DEATH,
    And again Death—ever Death, Death, Death,
    Hissing melodious, neither like the bird, nor like my
        aroused child's heart,
    But edging near, as privately for me, rustling at my
        feet,
    And creeping thence steadily up to my ears,
    Death, Death, Death, Death, Death.

34. Which I do not forget,
    But fuse the song of two together,
    That was sung to me in the moonlight on Paumanok's
        gray beach,
    With the thousand responsive songs, at random,
    My own songs, awaked from that hour,
    And with them the key, the word up from the waves,
    The word of the sweetest song, and all songs,
    That strong and delicious word which, creeping to
        my feet,
    The sea whispered me.

Whereto answering, the sea,   165
Delaying not, hurrying not,
Whisper'd me through the night, and very plainly before
    daybreak,
Lisp'd to me the low and delicious word death,
And again death, death, death, death,
Hissing melodious, neither like the bird nor like my
    arous'd child's heart,   170
But edging near as privately for me rustling at my feet,
Creeping thence steadily up to my ears and laving me
    softly all over,
Death, death, death, death, death.

Which I do not forget,
But fuse the song of my dusky demon and brother,   175
That he sang to me in the moonlight on Paumanok's gray
    beach,
With the thousand responsive songs at random,
My own songs awaked from that hour,
And with them the key, the word up from the waves,
The word of the sweetest song and all songs,   180
That strong and delicious word which, creeping to my feet,
(Or like some old crone rocking the cradle, swathed in
    sweet garments, bending aside,)
The sea whisper'd me.

Walt Whitman's New Poem*

The author of "Leaves of Grass" has perpetrated another "poem."
The N. Y. SATURDAY PRESS, in whose columns, we regret to say,
it appears, calls it "a curious warble." Curious, it may be; but
warble it is not, in any sense of that mellifluous word. It is a shade
less heavy and vulgar than the "Leaves of Grass," whose unmitigated
badness seemed to cap the climax of poetic nuisances. But the present
performance has all the emptiness, without half the grossness, of the
author's former efforts.

How in the name of all the Muses this so-called "poem" ever got
into the columns of the SATURDAY PRESS, passes our poor comprehension. We had come to look upon that journal as the prince of
literary weeklies, the *arbiter elegantiarum* of dramatic and poetic
taste, into whose well filled columns nothing stupid or inferior
could intrude. The numerous delicious poems; the sparkling *bons
mots*; the puns, juicy and classical, which almost redeemed that
vicious practice, and raised it to the rank of a fine art; the crisp
criticisms, and delicate dramatic humors of "Personne," and the
charming piquancies of the *spirituelle* Ada Clare—all united to make
up a paper of rare excellence. And it is into this gentle garden of the
Muses that that unclean cub of the wilderness, Walt Whitman, has
been suffered to intrude, trampling with his vulgar and profane
hoofs among the delicate flowers which bloom there, and soiling the
spotless white of its fair columns with lines of stupid and meaningless
twaddle.

Perhaps our readers are blissfully ignorant of the history and
achievements of Mr. Walt Whitman. Be it known, then, that he is a

---

* This review appeared in the *Cincinnati Daily Commercial* on December 28,
1859.

20

native and resident of Brooklyn, Long Island, born and bred in an obscurity from which it were well that he never had emerged. A person of coarse nature and strong, rude passions, he has passed his life in cultivating, not the amenities, but the rudenesses of character; and instead of tempering his native ferocity with the delicate influences of art and refined literature, he has studied to exaggerate his deformities, and to thrust into his composition all the brute force he could muster from a capacity not naturally sterile in the elements of strength. He has undertaken to be an artist, without learning the first principle of art, and has presumed to put forth "poems," without possessing a spark of the poetic faculty. He affects swagger and independence, and blurts out his vulgar impertinence under a full assurance of "originality."

In his very first performance, this truculent tone was manifested. He exaggerated every sentiment, and piled up with endless repetition every epithet, till the reader grew weary, even to nausea, of his unmeaning rant. He announced himself to the world as a new and striking thinker, who had something to reveal. His "Leaves of Grass" were a revelation from the Kingdom of Nature. Thus he screams to a gaping universe:

"I, Walt Whitman, an American, one of the roughs, a Cosmos; I shout my voice high and clear over the waves; I send my barbaric yawp over the roofs of the world!"

Such was the style of his performance, only it was disfigured by far worse sins of morality than of taste. Never, since the days of Rabelais was there such literature of uncleanness as some portions of this volume exhibited. All that is beautiful and sacred in love was dragged down to the brutal plane of animal passion, and the writer appeared to revel in language fit only for the lips of the Priapus of the old mythology.

We had hoped that the small reception accorded to his first performance had deterred Mr. Whitman from fresh trespasses in the realms of literature. Several years had passed away, his worse than worthless book had been forgotten, and we hoped that this Apollo of the Brooklyn marshes had returned to his native mud. But we grieve to say he revived last week, and although somewhat changed, changed very little for the better. We do not find so much that is offensive, but we do find a vast amount of irreclaimable drivel and inexplicable nonsense.

We have searched this "poem" through with a serious and deliberate endeavor to find out the reason of its being written; to discover some clue to the mystery of so vast an expenditure of words. But we honestly confess our utter inability to solve the problem. It is destitute of all the elements which are commonly desiderated in poetical composition; it has neither rhythm nor melody, rhyme nor reason, metre nor sense. We do solemnly assert, that there is not to be discovered, throughout the whole performance, so much as the glimmering ghost of an idea. Here is the poem, which the author, out of his characteristic perversity, insists upon calling the *Pre-verse*:

"Out of the rocked cradle.
Out of the mocking bird's throat,
The musical shuttle,
Out of the boy's mother's womb, and from the nipples of her breasts,
Out of the Ninth-Month midnight,
Over the sterile sea-sands, and the field beyond, where the child,
    leaving his bed, wandered alone, bareheaded, barefoot,
Down from the showered halo and the moonbeams,
Up from the mystic play of shadows twining and twisting as if they
    were alive,
Out from the patches of briars and blackberries,
From the memories of the bird that chanted to me,
From your memories, sad brother—from the fitful risings and
    fallings I heard,
From that night, infantile, under the yellow half-moon, late risen,
    and swollen as if with tears,
From those beginning notes of sickness and love, there in the mist,
From the thousand responses in my heart, never to cease,
From the myriad thence-aroused words,
From the word stronger and more delicious than any,
From such, as now they start, the scene revisiting,
As a flock, twittering, rising, or overhead passing,
Borne hither—ere all eludes me, hurriedly,
A man—yet by these tears a little boy again,
Throwing myself on the sand, I,
Confronting the waves, sing."

This is like nothing we ever heard of in literature, unless it be the following lucid and entertaining composition:

"Once there was an old women went into the garden to get some cabbage to make an apple pie. Just then a great she-bear comes up and pops his head into the shop. 'What, no soap!' So he died, and

she married the barber; and there was present at the wedding the
Jicaninies and the Piccaninies, and the Grand Panjandrum himself,
with a little round button at the top; and they all fell to playing the game
of catch as catch can, till the gun powder ran out of the heels of their
boots."

The "poem" goes on, after the same maudlin manner, for a hundred lines or more, in which the interjection "O" is employed above
five-and-thirty times, until we reach the following gem:

"Never again leave me to be the peaceful child I was before; what in
    the night,
By the sea, under the yellow and sagging moon,
The dusky demon aroused, the fire, the sweet hell within
The unknown want, the destiny of me."

O, but this is bitter bad!

"O give me some clue!
O if I am to have so much, let me have more!
O a word! O what is my destination?
O I fear it is henceforth chaos!"

There is not a doubt of it, we do assure you! And, what is more,
it never was anything else. Now, what earthly object can there be in
writing and printing such unmixed and hopeless drivel as that? If
there were any relief to the unmeaning monotony, some glimpse of
fine fancy, some oasis of sense, some spark of "the vision and the
faculty divine," we would not say a word. But we do protest, in the
name of the sanity of the human intellect, against being invited to
read such stuff as this, by its publication in the columns of a highly
respectable literary journal. What is the comment of the SATURDAY
PRESS itself on the "poem"? It says:

"Like the 'Leaves of Grass,' the purport of this wild and plaintive
song, well enveloped, and eluding definition, is positive and unquestionable, like the effect of music. The piece will bear reading many
times—perhaps, indeed, only comes forth, as from recesses, by many
repetitions."[1]

Well, Heaven help us, then, for as we are a living man, we would
not read that poem "many times" for all the poetry that was ever
perpetrated since the morning stars sang together. "Well enveloped,
and eluding definition." Indeed! We should think so. For our part,
we hope it will remain "well enveloped" till doomsday; and as for

[1] The reviewer is quoting from Whitman's prefatory note. [Ed.]

"definition," all we can do in that direction is to declare that either that "poem" is nonsense, or we are a lunatic.

If any of the tuneful Nine have ever descended upon Mr. Walt Whitman, it must have been long before that gentleman reached the present sphere of existence. His amorphous productions clearly belong to that school which it [is] said that neither gods nor men can endure. There is no meaning discoverable in his writings, and if there were, it would most certainly not be worth the finding out. He is the laureate of the empty deep of the incomprehensible; over that immortal limbo described by Milton, he has stretched the drag-net of his genius; and as he has no precedent and no rival, so we venture to hope that he will never have an imitator.

All About a Mocking-Bird*

What is the reason-why of Walt Whitman's lyric utterances, as soon as any of them is heard, rousing up such vehement intellectual censures and contumely from some persons, and then equally determined bravos from other persons?

Passing by certain of the latter, the complimentary sort, with which the journals, welcoming Walt's reappearance and recovery of his singing-voice after an obstinate three years' dumbness, have accepted that Mocking-Bird Chant printed by us in the *Saturday Press*, of Dec. 24, preceding, we seize upon and give to our readers, in another part of the paper, a specimen of the sort of censure alluded to—a tip-top cutting-and-slashing criticism from the *Cincinnati Daily Commercial*, which we have conned with unfeigned pleasure. All of which is respectfully submitted as outset for something else made way to be said, namely:

We feel authorized to announce, for certain, that the Mocking-Bird, having come to his throat again, his cantabile, is not going to give cause to his admirers for complaining that he idles, mute, any more, up and down the world. His songs, in one and another direction, will, he promises us, after this date, profusely appear.

We are able to declare that there will also soon crop out the true "Leaves of Grass," the fuller-grown work of which the former two issues were the inchoates—this forthcoming one, far, very far ahead of them in quality, quantity, and in supple lyric exuberance.

Those former issues, published by the author himself in little pittance-editions, on trial, have just dropped the book enough to ripple

---

* Printed in the *Saturday Press*, Vol. ii, no. 1 (January 7, 1860). Most critics agree that this defense of the poem is by Whitman which an analysis of style readily affirms.

the inner first-circles of literary agitation, in immediate contact with it. The outer, vast, extending, and ever-wider-extending circles, of the general supply, perusal, and discussion of such a work, have still to come. The market needs to-day to be supplied—the great West especially—with copious thousands of copies.

Indeed, "Leaves of Grass" has not yet been really published at all. Walt Whitman, for his own purposes, slowly trying his hand at the edifice, the structure he has undertaken, has lazily loafed on, letting each part have time to set,—evidently building not so much with reference to any part itself, considered alone, but more with reference to the ensemble,—always bearing in mind the combination of the whole, to fully justify the parts when finished.

Of course the ordinary critic, even of good eye, high intellectual calibre, and well accomplished, grasps not, sees not, any such ideal ensemble—likely sees not the only valuable part of these mystic leaves, namely, not what they state, but what they infer—scornfully wants to know what the Mocking-Bird means, who can tell?—gives credit only for what is proved to the surface—ear—and makes up a very fine criticism, not out of the soul, to which these poems altogether appeal, and by which only they can be interpreted, but out of the intellect, to which Walt Whitman has not, as far as we remember, addressed one single word in the whole course of his writings.

Then the workmanship, the art-statement and argument of the question. Is this man really any artist at all? Or not plainly a sort of naked and hairy savage, come among us, with yelps and howls, disregarding all our lovely metrical laws? How can it be that he offends so many and so much?

Quite after the same token as the Italian Opera, to most bold Americans, and all new persons, even of latent proclivities that very way, only accustomed to tunes, piano-noises and the performances of the negro bands—satisfied, (or rather fancying they are satisfied), with each and several thereof, from association and habit, until they pass utterly beyond them—which comes in good time, and cannot be deferred much longer, either, in such a race as yours, O bold American of the West!

Walt Whitman's method in the construction of his songs is strictly the method of the Italian Opera, which, when heard, confounds the new person aforesaid, and, as far as he can then see, showing no purport for him, nor on the surface, nor any analogy to his previous-accustomed tunes, impresses him as if all the sounds of earth and hell were tumbled promiscuously together. Whereupon he says what he candidly thinks (or supposes he thinks), and is very likely a first-rate fellow—with room to grow, in certain directions.

Then, in view of the latter words, bold American! in the ardor of youth, commit not yourself, too irretrievably, that there is nothing in the Italian composers, and nothing in the Mocking-Bird's chants. But pursue them awhile—listen—yield yourself—persevere. Strange as the shape of the suggestion may be, perhaps such free strains are to give to these United States, or commence giving them, the especial nourishments which, though all solid and mental and moral things are in boundless profusion provided, have hardly yet begun to be provided for them—hardly yet the idea of that kind of nourishment thought of, or the need of it suspected. Though it is the sweetest, strongest meat—pabulum of a race of giants—true pabulum of the children of the prairies.

You, bold American! and ye future two hundred millions of bold Americans, can surely never live, for instance, entirely satisfied and grow to your full stature, on what the importations hither of foreign bards, dead or alive, provide—nor on what is echoing here the letter and the spirit of the foreign bards. No, bold American! not even on what is provided, printed from Shakespeare or Milton—not even of the Hebrew canticles—certainly not of Pope, Byron, or Wordsworth, —nor of any German or French singer, nor any foreigner at all.

We are to accept those and every other literary and poetic thing from beyond the seas, thankfully, as studies, exercises. We go back— we pause long with the old, ever-modern one, the Homer, the only chanting mouth that approaches our case near enough to raise a vibration, an echo. We then listen with accumulated eagerness for those mouths that can make the vaults of America ring here to-day—those who will not only touch our case, but embody it and all that belongs to it—sing it with varied and powerful idioms, and in the modern spirit, at least as capable, as loud and proud as the best spirit that has ever preceded us.

Our own song, free, joyous, and masterful. Our own music, raised on the soil, carrying with it all the subtle analogies of our own associations—broad with the broad continental scale of the New World, and full of the varied products of its varied soils—composite—comprehensively Religious—Democratic—the red life-blood of Love, warming, running through every line, every word. Ah, if this Walt Whitman, as he keeps on, should ever succeed in presenting *such* music, *such* a poem, an identity, emblematic, in the regions of creative art, of the wondrous all—America, material and moral, he would indeed do something.

And if he don't, the Mocking-Bird may at least have the satisfaction of dying in a good cause. But then again he looks so little like dying, anyhow.

Floyd Stovall

From Main Drifts in Whitman's Poetry

. . .

In the second period of Whitman's poetical development, extending from 1859 to 1865, his barbaric yawp is silenced, and in its place are heard the softer song of love and the melancholy chant of death. These themes, illustrated in the key-poems, "Out of the Cradle Endlessly Rocking" and "When Lilacs Last in the Dooryard Bloom'd," which mark the beginning and conclusion respectively of the period, give to it a predominantly elegiac tone. The change from the joyous to the pensive mood, while not completed and confirmed until he had learned to forget himself in the army hospitals at Washington, had its origin probably in some more intimate experience that reached a crisis in 1859. "Out of the Cradle Endlessly Rocking," first published near the close of that year, has all the characteristics of a lament for the loss, by death or permanent separation, of a beloved companion and mistress. It is the first and only true love poem that Whitman ever wrote; this fact in itself gives it special significance. It is, moreover, his first poem that is tragic in tone and that is concerned seriously with death. It is difficult to account for this sudden change in mood except on the supposition of such an emotional upheaval as might be caused by the loss of a lover.

Some justification of this supposition is to be found in Whitman's numerous allusions, both in his poetry and in conversations reported by Horace Traubel, to a serious love entanglement with a woman of the South. On one occasion he told Traubel that he had "sacred, precious memories" of friends in the South; and at another time he spoke of "the one big factor, entanglement (I may almost say trag-

---

* Reprinted from *American Literature*, IV (March 1932), 8–10, by permission.

edy) of my life about which I have not so far talked freely with /9/ you."[1] We here see that though Whitman professed to have been intimate with more than one woman he remembers only one as a "big factor" in his life. The word "tragedy" is significant. He promised over and over to tell Traubel this big secret, but never did. So far as this poem is concerned, it does not matter whether or not Whitman had a normal sexual life; it may be, as many believe, that he was "romancing" in his famous letter to Symonds about his six children. Nevertheless he could have felt the agony of a bereaved lover, even as Poe felt it, and out of that agony produced a poem.[2]

Whether the experience that gave rise to it was real or imaginary, the poem unquestionably reveals a definite modification in the style and subject matter of *Leaves of Grass*. It has an intensity of feeling, a beauty of phrase and rhythm, and a definiteness of structure almost entirely lacking in Whitman's earlier work. In the experience here related he first discovered the true nature and meaning of the songs he should sing. The mocking bird is the symbol of the genius or daemon (spelled *demon* by Whitman) of the poet's soul.

> Demon or bird! (said the boy's soul,)
> Is it indeed toward your mate you sing? or is it really to me?
> For I, that was a child, my tongue's use sleeping, now I have
>   heard you,
> Now in a moment I know what I am for, I awake,
> And already a thousand singers, a thousand songs, clearer,
>   louder and more sorrowful than yours,
> A thousand warbling echoes have started to life within me,
>   never to die.

The child of the poem is perhaps symbolic of the immaturity of the poet of the first *Leaves*. The awakening here described certainly does not refer to his real childhood. Nor do I believe it refers to the original conception of *Leaves of Grass*, for the songs that the /10/ bird taught him were all sorrowful, whereas the first *Leaves* were joyous.

---

[1] Horace Traubel, *Walt Whitman in Camden*, II, 543.

[2] Emory Holloway thinks the poem was inspired by the death, shortly before the poem was composed, of a woman whom he loved. See *Walt Whitman: An Interpretation in Narrative*, p. 164.

Clara Barrus, in her recent book *Whitman and Burroughs: Comrades*, seems to think Whitman's story of six children a pathological fabrication (p. 337). Yet in a footnote (p. 338) she quotes from a letter from Whitman to Bucke, May 23, 1891, in which he said: "I have two deceased children (young man and woman—illegitimate of course) that I much desired to bury here with me—but have abandoned the plan on account of angry litigation and fuss generally, and disinterment from down South."

The songs are sorrowful because they spring from "unsatisfied love" which "the messenger there arous'd, the fire, the sweet hell within, the unknown want, the destiny of me." How shall this untold want be satisfied, the fire of unfulfilled love be quenched? Surely there is some solution, some solace for this pain, some hope that he can weave into his song. He looks to the sea, symbolic of the mystery of eternity, and pleads for a clue, a key-word, that will help him in his perplexity.

> Whereto answering, the sea
> Delaying not, hurrying not,
> Whisper'd me through the night, and very plainly before daybreak,
> Lisp'd to me the low and delicious word death,
> And again death, death, death, death,
> Hissing melodious, neither like the bird nor like my arous'd
>   child's heart,
> But edging near as privately for me rustling at my feet,
> Creeping thence steadily up to my ears and laving me softly all over,
> Death, death, death, death, death.

Death is the consoler, the clue to man's destiny, because it is the divine complement of human imperfection, through which love is made complete and immortal. The poignant emotions associated with this revelation awakened Whitman's latent aesthetic sense, and he turned away from his former poetry of theory and animal sensation and began to chant the sorrowful songs that now started to life within him, of which "Out of the Cradle Endlessly Rocking" was the first.

Henry Seidel Canby

Unifying Style in
"Out of the Cradle"*

. . .

The first stanza, admittedly beautiful, perfect in its flow, is an admirable example of how Whitman achieved a unifying style by definite methods of harmonizing expression which he chose in place of the familiarities of rhyme and metre.

First of all is what may be named perpendicular alliteration. Note the first word chosen for each line until the continuity of the pattern has been established: *out, out, out, over, down, up, out, from, from, from, from, from, from, from, from*. Next is interior alliteration, the repetition of the same consonant sound within the lines: here *m*, and *n*. Reading through one finds: *endlessly, mocking-bird, musical, Ninth-month, midnight, sands, and, beyond, wander'd, alone, down, from, mystic, twining, from, from, memories, chanted, me, from, memories, from, risings, fallings, from, under, moon, risen, swollen, from, beginnings, notes, yearning, in, mist, from, responses, my, never, from, myriad, thence, from, more, any, from, now, scene, rising, borne, me, man, again, myself, sand, confronting, chanter, pains, uniter, and, hints, them, them, reminiscence.*

And there is still a further alliterative (and rhyming) chain in the present participles—*rocking, mocking, leaving, twining, twisting, risings, fallings, beginning, yearning, revisiting, rising, passing, throwing, confronting, taking, leaping.*

More subtly, but with an equal effect of unity and continuity, is the nature of the line beginnings. They are pointing words; *out, over, down, up, from.* And the emphasis of position upon them is such as to make the movement of the poetry trochaic: *'Out of the, down*

---

* Reprinted from *Walt Whitman: An American—1943* (Boston: Houghton Mifflin Company, 1943), pp. 321–23, by permission. Title supplied by editor.

from the.' One must read *from* your memories, *from* those beginning, no matter what a futile scansion of the line into the supposed, but in English non-existent, 'feet' would indicate.

Thus the music and the continuity of style in this poem is established. So that the second stanza, beginning 'Once Paumanok, /322/ when the lilac-scent was in the air,' can pick up the *ins* and *ons,* and the participles with *growing,* and the pointing words with *up,* and the perpendicular alliteration with a new series: *and, and, and, and;* the internal alliteration with *every day, every day, every day,* and the trochaic feel of the measure with the emphasis upon *once, and, when, two, every,* and *cautiously.*

And thus, in a rhythmic and aural continuity, a poetic idea is expanded into a movement of verse. Nor should one fail to note the syntactical structure borrowed from oratorical rhetoric. The first stanza is all one sentence of balanced clauses, with its meaning suspended to the last word. This rhetorical characteristic of Whitman's style is again a device for unity, successful here, but often not successful. Periods, it may be said, usually appear in Walt's writing only when the breath is just about to give out!

I shall leave to the reader, if he is interested, the following-through of these devices to set the style and keep continuity in the rest of this perfectly composed poem, noting only, in the recitative, that the *m's* continue (surely the reason for bringing the *m*ocking-bird from Alaba*m*a).

Finally, the structure of the whole poem is as outstanding as the structure of a good essay. Its composition is complete, and the roman type and the italics indicate it. We have an introduction in recitative, a lyric beginning 'Shine! shine! shine!' a continuing narrative, a lyric 'Blow! blow! blow!' a meditation in recitative, a lyric 'Soothe! soothe! soothe!' in which the song is that of the boy's past but the love seems to be of the present as the intensity of the sexual imagery suggests, the waves embracing, lapping, the moon heavy with love, the sea pushing madly on the land. Here the purely lyric passages end with 'The aria sinking.' Whitman is conscious this time of the pattern of opera, and uses its vocabulary. The bird is identified in his fancy with a pure soprano reaching for the last tremulous notes, 'We two together no more.' And as in opera, the recitative again takes up the action, and so on to an elegy in which hopeless love is assuaged by the reconciliations of death.

I do not wish to labor this principle of unity in Whitman's style, and for this reason I make no attempt here to enter into /323/ subtler devices by which the intuitive poet gave form to his poetry of democracy which he thought must be freed from every shackle of convention. What he did, of course, was to try, as an innovator must, to find new binding forms for his chants—knowing well that even anarchy must have form if it is to be expressed. And where he failed, his poems crumble into a mass of lines—precisely as where his conventional contemporaries failed (Tennyson sometimes, Longfellow often), their poems become mere petrifications of words, held together by the silica of their techniques. The careful reader of the 'Leaves' will find that Whitman seldom failed in execution, but only in inspiration. When he thinks and feels prose, the structure loosens, weakens, gaps appear where there is only statement and no harmony, long catalogues are held together by a weak system of monotonous alliteration, or rhythmic similarity. But always, even when feeble, there is style.

Stephen E. Whicher

Whitman's *Out of the Cradle Endlessly Rocking**

Mr. Ralph D. Eberly is troubled by the apparent conflict between the "death-longing" and the "vigorous love of life" in "Out of the Cradle," and requests an analysis [EXP., Oct., 1946, V, Q2]. Perhaps the following comments will help to meet the difficulty.

The achievement of "Out of the Cradle" is a reconciliation of opposites. This it accomplishes, not by any "philosophy," but in an untranslatably poetical, not to say musical, way, by the development and association of themes and connotations.

The opposites it confronts, to speak far too abstractly and definitely, are Love and Death, the expansive principle of life and its negation. It is his awakening to *both* of these, through his response to the bird's song, that the poet chronicles; from this discovery of his humankindness he dates his poetic life. The theme is an optimistic version of the romantic favorite, the fall from innocence to experience, and the deepened spiritual life that compensates this loss.

The two principles do not emerge with equal plainness at the same stage in the poem. The awakening of the boy's capacity for love is unequivocal, but his response to the bird's sorrow is more obscure, as such adolescent emotion might well be. For all his ecstasy, he feels his security threatened, and seeks instinctively for new springs of courage to replace the peace he has outgrown. "What is my destination?" he asks. "Where can I turn?"

Here follows the poet's masterstroke, for the answer the sea brings is at the same time the key to the boy's trouble and the word that exercises it. Death is in truth at the root of the sorrow to which the

---

* Reprinted from *Explicator*, v (February, 1947), item 28, by permission. Copyright 1947 The Explicator.

bird's grief has also awakened him; yet "death" is the word with which the boy is consoled. This startling paradox, intellectually puzzling, is yet satisfying emotionally, precisely because it defeats expectations. Whitman prepares us for an affirmation, then substitutes a denial; the effect is to say, to the heart if not to the head, opposites meet; this *is* an affirmation; Death is Life.

The Life within nature that contradicts Death is established in the first introductory section; moon, shadows, night and sea are all instinct with life. The chief symbol of this is of course the sea, associated in the first line with birth and mother-love. Until the end of the bird's aria, this deeper life is held back, suggested chiefly in the rhythms. But at the end of the aria it awakens, along with the child's heart, and matches passion with passion. The sea, however, unlike the moon, is not made to respond in sentimental sympathy to the bird's grief. The "savage old mother" is indifferent to mere creaturely sorrows: here is something else, a deeper life beyond good and evil. Thus the way is paved for her paradoxical consolation.

The explicit personification of the sea as the World-Mother appears, of course, in the closing sections, when the boy first listens to the word she has been whispering throughout the poem. The motherly comfort, the security, the all-solving assurance of the sea's answer is suggested by every possible means, notably in the parenthetic picture at the end.

Yet the key word whispered by the old crone is Death. Does this represent a "death longing"? I believe such an interpretation is a misconception. The poem does not suggest that the problem of life is to be solved by death; it is death that is "solved." The "solution" is at bottom a matter of semantics. With all the emotional connotations of the passage pulling toward Love, the shock of the word "death" stirs the irresistible suggestion that death does not mean what we thought it did. A new ghost-sense more in harmony with the context, a mystical meaning compounded of Love, Life, and Birth, "uniter of here and hereafter," rises to envelope the literal sense, and transforms it *emotionally* into its opposite. The impact of the whole poem carries the literal sense by direct assault, and we are swept on in spite of ourselves into an irrational affirmation: Death, somehow, means Life. The powerful sense of release from limitations generated by this phoenix-like triumph of life lies at the heart of the poem's success.

The force of the poem thus depends on its being, as it is, everything to the heart and nothing to the intellect. Not that it doesn't stand up under analysis, for I think it does; but that it has no "meaning" and cannot be questioned. Its "meaning" is inseparable from its pattern of feeling, which is a self-sustaining whole. (The same pattern occurs in "When Lilacs Last.")

One is led to a further reflection: can it be said that the consolation by contradiction that governs this poem epitomizes a basic pattern of romantic feeling in America? It is in essence a Christian pattern, of course, a fall and a salvation by faith; it is a Christianity of the blood. Emerson spent his life teaching the same Christianity without dogma, and turned to much the same method of mystic contradiction: one less successful in his case, as it was on a more theoretic level, and so invited intellectual questions—a fatal fault. It is to be contrasted to the classic pattern of feeling, the tragic acceptance of limitations, exemplified in *Billy Budd.*

Roy P. Basler

Out of the Cradle
Endlessly Rocking*

Professor Whicher's suggestive analysis [EXP., Feb., 1947, V, 28] seems to me to enforce a mystical meaning that is not necessary, although not inappropriate, to the context. I should like to point out that a very simple reading may suffice; namely, that the poet's adolescent recognition of his own portion of "unsatisfied love" dates from his symbolic identification of his own meaning of the bird's song— that only death could finally assuage " . . . the fire, the sweet hell within, / The unknown want, the destiny of me." The assumption that the whole situation of the bird is symbolic of the boy's emotional problem (i.e., that the boy, too, has lost a companion or lover) is perhaps unwarranted by the established facts of Whitman's life, but that the bird's song of unsatisfied love, to which death is the only possible answer when no approved "object" is available, is symbolically apt for the boy's emotional dilemma (love which must for obvious reasons be suppressed or sublimated) seems simply appropriate. In this light, the concluding lines beginning "My own songs awaked from that hour" take on an appropriate personal significance which goes far toward providing an understanding of the recurrent theme of death as the answer to the soul's unsatisfied longing, which can be traced throughout Whitman's poetry to its culmination in "Good-Bye My Fancy," in which Whitman tenderly avows the only true recipient of his love during his long life as a creative artist. The prolongation in Whitman of an adolescent condition in which desire clamored for a fulfillment the object of which he could not at the time even imagine, may have been due to a recognized and re-

* Reprinted from *Explicator*, v (June, 1947), item 59, by permission. Copyright 1947 The Explicator.

jected tendency toward homosexuality. On the other hand, it may have been due to a mother-fixation. In any event, whether we accept the homosexual allusions elsewhere in Whitman's poetry as an avowal of fact or as a poetic symbolism, we cannot escape the fact that no object of his sexual attachment, of either sex, has been satisfactorily established by his biographers. "Out of the Cradle Endlessly Rocking" may be read as a poem recording the adolescent recognition of his necessity and the discovery of his poetic "self" through a symbolic experience which enabled the sublimation of desire to find expression in song.

Charles C. Walcutt

Whitman's "Out of the Cradle Endlessly Rocking"*

Whitman makes a statement about the springs of poetry in "Out of the Cradle," uniting all three levels—childhood memory, mature passion, and philosophical speculation—on which he speaks. On the first level, the poem describes a boyhood experience: the poet watched a mockingbird and his mate at their nest in the briars near the sea on Long Island. The she-bird disappears, and all summer long the he-bird sings a song of unsatisfied love. The poet "translates" this song, and at its completion the boy, ecstatic, weeping, "with his bare feet the waves, with his hair the atmosphere dallying/ The love in the heart long pent, now loose, now at last tumultuously bursting," grasps its meaning and the meaning of the experience, which is that he is to be a poet. This conclusion is elaborated in lines 144–59. The boy asks whether the bird is indeed a bird or his own spirit:

> Demon or bird! (Said the boy's soul,)
> Is it indeed toward your mate you sing? or is it really to me?

He welcomes the sudden knowledge of his "tongue's use" and the conviction that it will never cease uttering "the /278/ cries of unsatisfied love" and a thousand other songs more wonderful and sorrowful.

But all this appears rather sophisticated for a boy of ten-or-so years. It is unlikely that he should have so profound and immediate an understanding of the "cries of unsatisfied love." The explanation, of course, is that Whitman is not really writing about a boy's experience but about his own unsatisfied love. This second level of meaning

---

* Reprinted from *College English,* x (February, 1949), 277–79, with the permission of the National Council of Teachers of English and Charles C. Walcutt.

appears in the poem almost as early as the first: The "beginning notes of yearning and love" (l. II) suggest that more than a child's experience is involved; and the statement that the poet is a "uniter of here and hereafter" (l. 20) indicates that a mature intelligence is going to extend the application of the experience. When, before "translating" the bird's song of love, Whitman speaks of the "meanings which I of all *men* know" (l. 60; italics mine), he plainly reveals that an experience similar to the bird's has given him this special knowledge. These indications prepare for the long song of the bird which follows; it is rich in images of human love, mature human love, of a personal and sensual nature:

> Close on its wave soothes the wave behind,
> And again another behind embracing and lapping, every one close, . . .
>
> O madly the sea pushes upon the land,
> With love, with love [ll. 72–73, 77–78].

Now, if these metaphors clearly indicate that the boy's experience is a symbol through which a mature experience of unsatisfied love is presented, the question arises whether the loosing of his poetic utterance is to be thought of as coming from the boy's or the man's experience. And again it appears that the real subject of the poem is a thwarted love and that it was by this that the poetic faculty was stimulated. Whitman speaks of himself as a "peaceful child" (l. 154). A peaceful child would not be deeply stirred by a bird's song. The song would only reveal or resolve emotional tensions already existing. The man, tormented by desire and unable to satisfy his passion, might conceivably be aided in surmounting and transcending his condition by a further experience. Whether the bird's song can be taken as symbolic of such an experience or not, it is not a speaking symbol. One might as safely assume that the passage of time enabled the poet to transmute an intense but limiting passion into the substance of poetic insight.

This is indeed the central truth in the poem. The climax comes with the lines, "The aria sinking, / All else continuing . . ." where a colloquy is held between the boy, the bird, and the sea, and the boy has an ecstatic experience of insight into the nature of reality. (In l. 137 Whitman speaks of "the love in the heart long pent, now loose, now at last tumultuously bursting," and in l. 154 of "the peaceful child." This slight contradiction allows the real subject for a moment to appear without its mask. The boy was peaceful; the man, tormented.)

The third or philosophical level dominates the poem after the climax. From this single, intense, mystical experience comes the promise of a "thousand songs." One experience has unlocked innumerable doors; the man's life is transformed by a new insight. And the new poet asks quite specifically how this can have happened—how it was possible for one experience to lead into so much:

> O give me the clew! (it lurks in the night here somewhere,)
> O if I am to have so much, let me have more!

The sea answers with the "strong and delicious word" *death.* How does the word /279/ "death" answer the poet's question? There are at least two possible explanations:

1. Whitman realizes that the immediate object of a personal love will have to be removed if that love is to transcend into a perception of the thousand truths of which his songs will tell. The particular is seen as a key to the universal when the particular is removed and the individual is freed to contemplate universals. As Thoreau says, "The rays which stream through the shutter will be no longer remembered when the shutter is wholly removed."

2. The word "death," uttered by the sea, is the sea's revelation of its own secret, which is the Unity of Being. It is because reality is One that a single intense vision into truth can be a key to innumerable insights. Emerson said that the universe is contained in every one of its particles. Whitman made a powerful metaphor on the physical unity of being in the lines of "Crossing Brooklyn Ferry":

> I too was struck from the float forever held in solution,
> I too had receiv'd identity by my body,
> That I was I knew was of my body, and what I should
> be I knew I should be of my body.

The "float" is a liquid in which all substance is dissolved, so that every drop of the float contains all that the whole is. An individual "struck from the float" is like a drop crystallized (or precipitated) into form. This figure is a rendering of Emerson's transcendentalism with a material rather than a "spiritual" emphasis. It is not surprising, then, that the sea should be for Whitman[2] a symbol of what

---

[2] Using the poet's name as I have, I may appear to be confusing biography and poetry, a confusion that is more tempting in the exegesis of Whitman's poems than in those of almost any other poet. But since Whitman created a more or less fictitious personality for his poems, I believe we can without confusion discuss the poems as the dramatization of this fictitious Whitman—without reference to the biography of the actual man.

Emerson designates as Spirit. Now, because all experiences are versions of the one Experience, it is possible for any one to be a key to all the rest. This is the answer the poet asks for in the poem; and this answer is given by the sea in the word "death." Death is the process by which separate individuals are returned to the unity of material being. Death is the constant evidence of this unity. But the word "death," as the sea utters it, is not a fact of someone's dying but an idea of Unity. It is a "strong and delicious word" for the poet. I do not believe that Whitman's use of the word "death" here indicates, as has been said, a new "spirituality" in which "death is the divine complement of human imperfection." Can it not be entirely a symbol, standing not for the passage of the soul to immortality but for an understanding (or intuition) of the eternal unity of Being—a unity that can be grasped by the living human reason and that does not have to wait for the death of the individual?

Leo Spitzer

Explication de Texte Applied to Walt Whitman's Poem "Out of the Cradle Endlessly Rocking"*†

I may state first that our poem treats the age-old theme of world harmony within which the bird is one voice, the sea another, and the poet the third. The classical and Christian ideas of world harmony have been treated by me in *Traditio* (II and III, 1945–6) and it may be apposite for me to extract from this article a brief survey: Pythagoras and Plato had defined music as an art practiced not only by human musicians, but also by the cosmos. According to Plato's *Timaeus*, the music of the spheres is produced by Sirens each of whom, in her particular sphere, sings notes whose pitch is conditioned by the velocity of the revolution of her sphere. The totality of these notes produces that world harmony, or symphony inspired by loving rivalry, ἔρις καὶ φιλία, which is inaccessible to human ears, and which is willed by the demiurge, the world spirit. It was not difficult for the Christians to replace the pagan world spirit by the Christian God of Love and thus to associate the music of the spheres with Christian *Caritas*. In Dante, the Pythagorean world harmony will be sung, not by the Sirens of the *Timaeus* but by the pure intelligences,

---

* Reprinted from *Journal of English Literary History*, XVI (September, 1949), 229–49, by permission of The Johns Hopkins Press.

† Since I have no thorough acquaintance with Walt Whitman's sources, I am forced to place him, not within the framework of his American *ambiente*, but somewhere in the cold space of world literature (as far as I know it), to treat the poem "Out of the Cradle Endlessly Rocking" as one among other poetic monuments belonging to the Western tradition, apart from the question of Whitman's familiarity or non-familiarity with these monuments. My ignorance, however, may in the end be redeemed to some degree: for I feel that the direct, concrete sources which may be established for a particular work of art, are generally somewhat petty and trivial in comparison with the parallels to be found in international art, together with which the particular work combines in an eternal pattern. I have used Stovall's *Walt Whitman*, N. Y. 1934.

43

the angels vying with each other in the different revolving heavens through the physical and spiritual attraction of that Divine Love "che muove il sole e le altre stelle." Already Augustine had seen the world as a "magnum (musicum) carmen creatoris et moderatoris." The theme that the music of nature blends with /230/ human voices in praise of the Lord is first developed in an exegetic text of Saint Ambrose, intended to interpret the line of *Genesis* in which God is presented as satisfied with his creation of the sea. In surging prose Ambrose offered a powerful acoustic description of the harmony (*concentus* = συμφωνία) in which are fused the song of the waves and the choirs of the devout congregation in an island sanctuary: the voices of men, women, children chanting psalms. "Quam dulcis sonus, quam jucundus fragor ('refraction'), quam grata et consona resultatio (= 'harmonious echo') !" With Ambrose we find for the first time in our occidental literatures the fusion of nature and humanity into one *Stimmung*, into a unity of tone and atmosphere prompted by Christian feelings. It is this transcendental unity which permits the single objects to lose their matter-of-fact identity and to melt into the general atmosphere of piety; whereas in the pantheism of the ancients, though the single phenomenon may even change into another form (as in the metamorphoses of Philomela or Echo), clear-cut forms still continue to exist individually, not fused into an all-embracing atmosphere.

After Ambrose we find birds presented in Latin medieval poetry as psalmists of God, Nature's singers introduced into the more sophisticated company of human singers. Among these birds the nightingale figures predominantly. The classical Philomela, the ravished, mutilated, sorrowing woman-become-songbird (in accord with the ancient tendency to explain the healing effect of music by tragic suffering overcome), becomes in Christian poetry the singer, naturally endowed with divine Grace, who sings to testify to Grace. In a tenth-century Latin poem the nightingale sings at Eastertime, inviting all believers to join with her in praise of the resurrected Christ. From now on medieval love songs reflecting the theological theme begin with a picture of nature revived in spring, with the birds and the poet vying in grateful song (the *Natureingang* of the Minnesingers and troubadours). The word *refrain* (lit. 'refraction'), which in Old French was applied to the twittering of birds as well as to the musical or verbal *refrain*, must be explained by the concept of the echo which is represented in the response of the birds to the music of the world. Similarly, the /231/ modern word *concert* (lit. 'musical contest'), and the Elisabethan word *consort* ('concert') = *consortium* ('association'), are late derivatives from this same idea of peaceful strife, of musically

harmonious emulation in the praise of God. The thirteenth-century
Spanish poet Gonzalo de Berceo goes so far as to portray learned birds
that serve as preachers of religious orthodoxy. Church-fathers and
prophets of the Old Testament, Augustine, Saint Gregory, and Isaiah,
are presented as nightingales in an earthly paradise competing under
the dictation of the Virgin Mary. A one-man concert is Saint Francis'
famous canticle: "Altissimo onnipotente bon signore, / tue so le laude,
la gloria e l'onore e onne benedizione." This minstrel of God, feeling
that one human being alone would not be worthy of praising the
Lord, brings into his poem all creatures which may testify with him
to the greatness of the Creator: "Messer lu frate Sole" (the Lord my
brother Sun), my brother the wind, my sister the water, my sister the
earth—and my sister Death. According to legend, the last stanza was
added by Saint Francis on the day of his death. The Saint does not
mention his brother the bird, but we remember the painting of
Giotto in which Francis is depicted as preaching to the birds.

In the Renaissance, the original classical concept of Pythagorean
and Platonic World Harmony was revived by poets and scholars:
Marsilio Ficino, Kepler (*Harmonices mundi*), and others. The Christian implications, however, which had come to be associated in the
Middle Ages with that ancient theory, were not disregarded by the
Platonists whether Catholic or Protestant. This we see in the *Musur-
gia* of the Jesuit Athanasius Kircher and in the writings of the
Protestant Leibnitz. Thus when Shakespeare stresses the unmusical
in Shylock or Cassius, he means that these characters are untouched
by Christian grace. The Renaissance painter *par excellence*, Raphael,
shows us Saint Cecilia, surrounded by such figures as Saint Augustine
and Saint Mary Magdalen (the Christian theoretician of music and
the representative of love rewarded by grace), in a moment of ecstasy
when she, an earthly being, gifted for music, or endowed with grace,
is privileged to hear the music of heaven. Dryden's "Song for St.
Cecilia's Day" and Milton's "At a Solemn Music" celebrate the reunion in /232/ heaven with God's music from which we earthly singers have been estranged through original sin.

> Disproportioned sin
> Jarr'd against nature's chime, and with harsh din
> Broke the fair *music that all creatures made*
> To their great Lord.
> O may we soon again renew that song,
> And keep in tune with Heav'n till God ere long
> To his celestial consort us unite,
> To live with him, and sing in endless morn of light.

To die with the expectance of heavenly, Pythagorean-Christian music
is sweet. Not only the sweetness of musical reunion with Christ, but
the sweetness of a musical death for Christ is expressed by a seven-
teenth-century German mystic Friedrich von Spee who, in a language
that has the simplicity of the folksong, gives a baroque twist to the
classical motif of the tragic death of Philomela. He combines this
motif with that of the Echo that we found in Ambrose, although the
scenery here is not the all-embracing ocean, but a German forest. A
nightingale exultantly sings out the name of Christ to which the echo
responds with equal enthusiasm:

> Da recht, du fromme Nachtigal,
> Du jenem Schall nit weiche,
> Da recht, du treuer Widerschall,
> Du stets dich ihr vergleiche,
> Zur schönen Wett'
> Nun beide trett,
> Mein Jesum lasst erklingen.

Then the 'risings and fallings' of the two voices that descend in order
to ascend to ever-higher pitch suddenly cease. The nightingale has
died in the praise of "mein Jesum,"—a martyr of love and strife for
God.

The English Romantics introduce into poetry their selves and their
problems of disenchantment, caused by the waning of faith in the
eighteenth century. Now the poet is isolated from the musical birds;
no concert materializes. Shelley is startled to hear a lone nightingale
"answering him with soothing song" when he sits "pale with grief
beneath the tower." Or else he will address the skylark: "*Teach* us,
Sprite or Bird, What sweet thoughts are thine. . . Teach me half the
gladness / That /233/ thy brain must know." The bird is here a
teacher as in medieval poetry, but not a teacher of a firmly established
orthodoxy which is shared by bird and poet alike, nor a brother in
the love of God. The teaching which the poet requests of the strange
visitor ("sprite or bird") from another world is apparently concerned
with the knowledge of ultimate things inaccessible to the poet. Keats
who apostrophizes the Nightingale ("Thou wert not born for death,
immortal bird") feels himself to be immediately thrown back "from
thee to my sole self," and as the bird's voice fades away, the poet is
left, unlike his medieval confrère, in "forelorn" uncertainty. Was this
a vision or a dream?

The German pre-Romantics and Romantics do not express the feeling of basic isolation from nature. On the contrary, the Germans
wished to recognize themselves in articulate nature. Along with the

discovery of folk poetry and of Ossian there went the resurrection of
those elemental spirits or sprites, those degraded demi-gods of an-
tiquity who, in spite of the ban of the Church, had been able to survive in popular superstition and in whom were incarnated the
irrational cosmic fears of man and the daemoniac magic by which
man may be seduced at any moment. Whereas Plato's Sirens sang
their symphonic chorus in accord with a Pythagorean mathematical
order, now the sirens of the folklore, the daemoniac daughters of the
Erlkönig in Herder and Goethe sing to lure innocent children away
from their parents. The mermaid by her singing and pleading at-
tracts the fisherman toward the abyss (Goethe, *Der Fischer*: "Sie
sang zu ihm, sie sprach zu ihm, da war's um ihn geschehn"), and
Heine's *Loreley*, by dint of singing and combing her fair German
hair, sends the boatsman down to the deep. Thus, as man, gradually
dechristianized, realizes his own daemoniac nature—we may remember Goethe's belief in his (and Napoleon's) *daimonion*—, an ambiguous folkloristic religion of underworld Gods tends to replace the truly
religious world of order and clarity that had produced the concept
of musical world harmony. But though the orderly picture of the
world has faded by the eighteenth century, the original desire of the
individual to fuse somehow with nature has survived, particularly
with the Germans, who always feel their own individu- /234/ ality
to be somehow incomplete. This desire may assume two forms: the
pantheistic and the religious. Werther, so much torn in his feelings,
is never shaken in his craving for pantheistic union with nature; in
fact, to integrate with the whole of nature is the purpose of his sui-
cide. The religious variant is represented by Eichendorff. This Catholic poet is not a narcissistic intellectual mirroring himself in nature,
but an unproblematic, gaily bird-like being, somewhat puerile perhaps, but living in unison with the aimless beauty of the world. No
German poet has identified himself so thoroughly with the German
forest and its denizens. He speaks in the first person in the name of
the skylark which sings bathed in sunlight, feeling its breast bursting
with song. His nightingale is called upon to announce the meaning
of his poetic universe:

> ... in der Einsamkeit verkünde
> was sie alle, alle meinen:
> dieses Rauschen in den Bäumen
> und der Mensch in dunkeln Träumen.

The rustling of the dusky leaves of the forest as well as the dark confused dreams of man carry the same message: the affirmation of the

aimlessness of nature (human and non-human), whose inexplicability should be respected. It remained for the French Romantics, the seraphic Lamartine and the gigantic Victor Hugo, to celebrate pantheistic world harmony with their French articulateness, with the rhetorical grandiloquence and sonority of their voices. One was the flute, the other the organ. Victor Hugo's Satyr (*Le satyre*) dethrones the serene Gods of the Olympus and reveals himself with a stentorian voice as Pan, before whom Jove must abdicate. There is no doubt that Hugo saw himself as that animal-God, as the incarnation of a strange Gallo-Greek earthiness which owes more to Rabelais than to Theocritus. Never since the time of the early Christian hymns had one heard such powerful songs of world-harmony nor since the time of Horace such strong affirmation of the rôle of the poet as *vates*, as Bard. In 1830 Victor Hugo writes:

> C'est que l'amour, la tombe, et la gloire, et la vie,
> L'onde qui fuit par l'onde incessamment suivie,
> Tout souffle, tout rayon, ou propice ou fatal,
> Fait reluire et vibrer mon âme de cristal,
> Mon âme aux mille voix, que le Dieu que j'adore
> Mit au centre de touch comme un écho sonore. /235/

The poet himself is both the echo and the crystal placed in the center of the universe by a God whom he, so to speak, crowds out. Victor Hugo is the almighty sensorium that unites, reflects, and speaks for the whole of creation. Obviously the tiny voice of a bird would be superfluous in the concert of thousand voices, or in the pandemonium set in motion by the Bard alone. For, unlike Saint Francis, Hugo believes that the poet may give voice to the world concert. Less optimistically and more modestly, de Musset saw in the poet the voice of suffering incarnate; he offers humanity his bleeding heart for food as the pelican does to her young. "Les plus désespérés sont les chants les plus beaux, / Et j'en sais d'immortels qui sont de purs sanglots." For Baudelaire the poet is the albatross, an exile from heaven plodding clumsily on this earth. Similarly for Mathew Arnold Philomela is a "wanderer from a Grecian shore" and her song is, as in Greek times, "eternal passion, eternal pain." The function of the Hugoian "sonorous world-echo" was taken over in the second half of the nineteenth century by the greatest sorcerer-artist of all times, the musician Richard Wagner. With him operatic art is used to express the will to love and death, which, according to Schopenhauerian philosophy, animates all of creation, man and nature alike. The opera which had

been created in the Baroque period as a demonstration of the soothing power of music on all creatures—it is not chance that Orpheus,
the tamer of animals and the conqueror of hell, was its original main
protagonist—is called upon by Wagner to express the religion of the
nineteenth century: pantheism, the voice of the forest in *Siegfried*,
of fire in the *Walküre* and of the individual striving for dissolution
in death in *Tristan and Isolde*. Wagner gave to his concept of world
harmony an orchestration which interpreted the togetherness of
voices in the world, each singing its own *unendliche Melodie*, in a
novel density of design and compactness of texture which has over-
powered millions of listeners on a scale never attained by any artist
working with the medium of sound.

After this rapid and over-simplified survey it should have become
clear that in the poem "Out of the Cradle" Whitman has offered a
powerful original synthesis of motifs which have been elaborated
through a period of 1500 years of Occidental /236/ poetry. The
poems I have mentioned are not necessarily his immediate material
sources; but I am convinced that his "bird or demon" is a descendant
of Shelley's "Sprite bird," that the brother mocking-bird is one of
Saint Francis' brother creatures, that his "feathered guests from Alabama" is a derivate from Arnold's "wanderer from a Grecian shore,"
that the conception of "a thousand singers, a thousand songs . . . a
thousand echoes" all present in the poet is a rëelaboration of Victor
Hugo's "âme aux mille voix" and "écho sonore." Be this as it may,
the basic motifs in which the idea of world harmony has taken shape
in Europe must be in our mind when we read Whitman's poem, which
becomes greater to the degree that it can be shown as ranking with,
and sometimes excelling, the great parallel poems of world literature.

Our poem is organized in three parts: a *prooemium* (l. 1–22), the
tale of the bird (l. 23–143), and the conclusion in which the influence
of the bird on the 'outsetting bard' is stated (l. 144— to the end).
Parts one and three correspond to each other and occasionally offer
parallel wording.

The proem, composed in the epic style of *arma virumque cano*,
not only defines the theme of the whole poem clearly but translates
this definition into poetry. The proem consists of one long, "oceanic"
sentence which symbolizes by its structure the poetic victory achieved
by the poet: "Out of the Cradle . . . down . . . up . . . out . . . from . . .
I, chanter of pains and joys, uniter of here and hereafter . . . A reminiscence sing.' Out of the maze of the world, symbolized by those
numerous parallel phrases, introduced by contrasting prepositions,
which invite the inner eye of the reader to look in manifold direc-

tions, though *out of* and *from* predominate—out of the maze of the world emerges the powerful Ego, the "I" of the poet, who has extricated himself from the labyrinth (his victory being as it were sealed by the clipped last line "a reminiscence sing").

The longer the sentence, the longer the reader must wait for its subject, the more we sense the feeling of triumph once this subject is reached: the Ego of the poet that dominates the cosmos. It is well known that this is the basic attitude of Walt Whitman toward the world. "Walt Whitman, a kosmos, of Manhattan the son, turbulent, fleshy, sensual . . .", he says in the "Song of Myself." He felt himself to be a microcosm re- /237/ flecting the macrocosm. He shares with Dante the conviction that the Here and the Hereafter collaborate toward his poetry, and as with Dante this attitude is not one of boastfulness. Dante felt impelled to include his own human self (with all his faults) because in his poem his Ego is necessary as a representative of Christendom on its voyage to the Beyond.[1] Walt Whitman felt impelled to include in his poetry his own self (with all his faults) as the representative of American democracy undertaking this worldly voyage of exploration. "And I say to mankind, Be not curious about God. . . I see God each hour of the twenty-four, . . . In the faces of men and women I see God, and in my own face in the glass." "I am of old and young, of the foolish as much as the wise, one of the Nation of many nations . . . A Southerner soon as a Northerner . . . Of every hue and caste am I, of every rank and religion."[2] But in contrast to Dante who knew of an eternal order in this world as in the Beyond, Whitman finds himself faced with an earthly reality whose increasing complexity made correspondingly more difficult his achievement of poetic mastery. Therefore Whitman must emphasize more his personal triumph. The complexity of the modern world finds its usual

---

[1] Cf. my "Note on the poetic and empirical 'I' in medieval authors" in *Traditio* IV, 414.

[2] Whitman has expressed the necessity of his Ego for his poetry in the following prose lines of his "Backward glance o'er travel'd roads": "I saw, from the time my enterprise and questionings positively shaped themselves (how best can I express my own distinctive era and surroundings, America, Democracy?) that the trunk and centre . . . must be an identical body and soul, a personality—which personality, after many considerations and ponderings, I deliberately settled should be myself— indeed could not be any other . . . 'Leaves of Grass,' indeed . . . has mainly been . . . an attempt, from first to last, to put *a person*, a human being (myself in the latter half of the Nineteenth Century, in America,) freely, fully and truly on record." Whitman could not realize that he was repeating Dante's procedure, that the poet of democracy must impersonate this sublime abstraction with the same consistency that made Dante impersonate the universal Christian quest for the Beyond. The sea must whisper its oracle 'privately' to Whitman just as Beatrice in the Beyond calls Dante by his personal name.

expression with Whitman in the endless catalogues, so rarely understood by commentators: in what I have called his "chaotic enumeration" ("La enumeración caótica en las literaturas modernas," Buenos
Aires 1945), a device, much imitated after him by Rubén Darís,
Claudel, and Werfel. This poetic device consists of lumping together
things spiritual and physical, as the raw material of our rich, /238/
but unordered modern civilization which is made to resemble an
oriental bazaar. In this poem it is only one specific situation whose
material and spiritual ingredients Whitman enumerates: the natural
scene (Paumanok beach at night), the birds, the sea, the thousand
responses of the heart of the boy-poet, and his "myriad thence-arous'd
words,"—they are all on one plane in this poem, no one subordinated
to another, because this arrangement corresponds to Whitman's chaotic experience. Similarly the two temporal planes, the moment
when the boy felt the "myriad words" aroused in him on Paumanok
beach, and the other when the mature poet feels the rise of "the
words such as now start the scene revisiting," are made to coincide
because, at the time of the composition of the poem, they are felt as
one chaotic but finally mastered experience: the boy who observed
the birds now has become the poet. When defining his creative rôle
here in the poem, Whitman does not indulge in chaotic enumeration
of his qualities as he does in the passage from the "Song of Myself"
in which he appears as a Protean demigod. Now he presents himself
simply and succinctly as: "I, chanter of pains and joys, uniter of here
and hereafter." Out of hydralike anarchy he has created unity; and,
as we see, he has gained not only an emotional, but an intellectual
triumph; he represents himself as "taking all hints, but swiftly leaping beyond them" like a master philologian or medieval glossator
(later he will insist on his rôle as cautious "translator of the birds'
cry," 31 and 69). Whitman takes care to impress upon us the intellectual side of the synthesis he has achieved; a claim that is not unjusti-
fied and an aspect that should be stressed more in a poet in whose
work generally only the sensuous and chaotic aspect is emphasized.

His "uniting" powers have been revealed to us in his first stanza;
in fact in the first line of the poem which gives it its title. With its
rocking rhythm, the line suggests the cradle of the infinite sea from
which later, at the end of the poem, *death* will emerge. At this stage,
however, death is already a part of the situation. It is present in the
phrase "From a word stronger and more delicious than any," which
the reader is not yet able to understand. Now we can visualize only
the ocean, the main instrument in the concert of world harmony with
which the /239/ song of the bird and the thousand responses of the
poet fuse. Whitman restores the Ambrosian fullness and the unity of

Stimmung of the world concert of love, music, and ocean (but obviously without Ambrose's theism). There will be no dainty *Vogel-
konzert* in a German romantic nook, no dolorous dialogue between
a soul estranged from nature and a bird-sprite in an English country-
side; the American ocean, "the savage old mother" will provide the
background and the undertone to the whole poem. In this Ambrosian
concert of world harmony we may distinguish also the Hugoian voice
of the poet consisting of a thousand voices; but the insistent repetitions "a thousand singers, a thousand echoes" give rather the effect
of a struggle on the poet's part, a struggle with the infinite, than that
of a complacent equation ("I am the universe!") such as we find in
Hugo.

After the organ- and tuba-notes that resound in the proem, the
tone changes entirely in the main part, which is devoted to the reminiscence proper, to the singing of the mocking-birds and the listening
of the boy. Here we find a straightforward narrative interrupted by
the lyrical songs or "arias" of the birds. Given the setting of nature
within which the boy and the bird meet, the term *aria* (130, 138)
with its operatic, theatrical connotation as well as the musicological
term *trio* (140) that immediately follows (applied to the ears, the
tears, and the soul of the boy), may seem too *précieux*. In *Song of
Myself*, we recall, Whitman speaks of the tree-toad as "a *chef-d'oeuvre*
for the highest." But we must also remember that Whitman's world-
embracing vision is able to contain in itself opposite aspects of the
world at once together. In this vision the manmade or artificial has
its genuine place near the product of nature and may even be only
another aspect of the natural. The song of the mocking-bird, so
naturally sweet, is an artefact of nature that teaches the human artist
Whitman.[3]

To return to our narrative, this offers us a development in time of
the theme that had been compressed to one plane in /240/ the
proem: the boy become poet. In such a development, we would ex-
pect, according to conventional syntax, to find the historical flow of
events expressed by verbs. But to the contrary, this narrative section
offers throughout an almost exclusively nominal style, that is, the
coupling of nouns with adjectives or participles, without benefit of
finite verbs or copulas. This is an impressionistic device known in
French as "écriture artiste," which was introduced by the Goncourts

---

[3] But we should keep in mind that Whitman's pantheistic unification of the
cosmos, as is true of all similar modern attempts, is informed by a pantheism that
comes *after* Christianity, a pantheism-that-has-absorbed-Christianity. The Christian
feeling for the unity of the world in God can never be lost in modern times, not
even when God Himself is lost.

in their diary in the 1850's; for example, "Dans la rue. Tête de femme aux cheveux retroussés en arrière, dégageant le bossuage d'un front étroit, les sourcils remontés vers les tempes . . . ; un type physique curieux de l'énergie et de la volonté féminines" (*Journal des Goncourt*, [1856], I 134). This we call impressionistic because with the suppression of the verb the concatenation and development of happenings gives way to the listing of unconnected ingredients, or, in pictorial terms, to touches of color irrespective of the units to which the colored objects belong. Accordingly, we find with Whitman: "Once Paumanok . . . two feathered guests . . . and their nest . . . and every day the he-bird to and fro . . . and every day . . . I cautiously peering . . .", a procedure that is brought to a high point of perfection in that masterpiece of the last stanza of the second part: "The aria sinking, all else continuing, the stars shining . . . The boy ecstatic . . . The love in the heart long pent . . ." I see in these participles nervous notations of the moment which serve not to reenact actions, but to perpetuate the momentary impressions which these have made on the boy when he was perceiving them. When the boy sensed that the melancholy song was subsiding, he jotted down in the book of memory the words: "Aria sinking," and we the readers may still perceive that first nervous reaction. The development of the boy is then given the style appropriate to a "reminiscence." The style here chosen is such as to impress upon us the fragmentary nature of the naked "reminiscence." Because of the non-finite form of the participles, single moments are forever arrested, but, owing to the verbal nature of these forms, the moment is one of movement, of movement crystallized. Of course, such vivid rendering of a reminiscence is possible only in languages, such as /241/ English or Spanish, that possess the progressive form, of which the simple participle may represent the elliptical variant.[4]

---

[4] One will notice that in the sentence quoted above from the *Journal des Goncourt* the style of the diary is applied to a static picture, not to an action in the making. *Dégageant le bossuage* stands in attributive relationship to *tête de femme* whereas *sinking* offers a predication about *the aria* (in other words, *the aria sinking* contains a double beat). Moreover, the participles of the Goncourts are all grouped under one heading *tête de femme* finally summed up as *un type physique* . . . , whereas in Whitman's stanza we have a list of different actions, all of equal weight. Accordingly, the Goncourt passage offers a tighter sentence structure. This quality was evidently perceived by Lanson who, in his *Art de la prose*, p. 265, discussing this passage, remarks of the *Journal* in general: "Ce Journal est très *écrit*; on n'y sent jamais l'abandon, la furie de la notation improvisée." There is then a pose of diary-writing in the Goncourts. With Whitman, on the contrary, the sequence of nominal sentences gives the effect of genuinely improvised notation, such as the boy himself might actually have made at the moment in *his* 'note-book,' the book of memory.

Now, from line 138 on, while the initial rhythm of the stanza
seems to continue, there appear strange inversions such as "The aria's
meaning, the ears, the soul, swiftly depositing" (for "the ears, the
soul swiftly depositing the aria's meaning" and similarly in 140 and
141), inversions quite unusual in English, even jarring upon the
English *Sprachgefühl*. We must evidently suppose that the "extasis"
(l. 136) of the boy is working in an effort comparable to travail toward an intellectual achievement. It is "the aria's *meaning*" that is
now being found by him and the jarring construction is the "impressionistic" rendering of the difficulty with which this inner event is
made to happen. It has already been noted that the activities here
reflected by the sequence of participles and other modifiers are all of
equal weight. We have not yet stressed the extent to which the
"enumerative" procedure has been carried out in our stanza, which
indeed consists only of detached phrases of the type "the . . . .-ing
(-ed) ." The chaotic enumeration offered us here is intended to show
the collaboration of the whole world ("all else," "the stars," "the
winds," "the fierce old mother," "the yellow half-moon," "the boy
extatic," "the love," "the ears, the soul," "the strange tears," "the
colloquy, the trio," and "the undertone of the sea") toward that
unique event—the birth of a poet out of a child who has grasped
the meaning of the world. The nervous, impressionistic enumeration
is symbolic of the travail of this birth. On the other hand, the repetition in this whole stanza of the atonic rhyme -*ing*, an /242/ ending
that appeared already in the first line with the suggestion of *rocking*,
evokes the all-embracing rhythm and permanent undertone or counterpoint of the sea, whether fiercely howling or softly rocking, as it
comes to drown out the chamber-music, the *trio* of ears, soul and
tears in the boy. The rhyme in -*ing* is a *leitmotif* that orchestrates
the arias of boy and bird and gives the poem a Wagnerian musical
density of texture.

As for the songs of the birds, let us note first that Whitman has
chosen to replace the hackneyed literary nightingale by a domestic
bird of America, the mocking-bird, compared to which, Jefferson
once declared, the European nightingale is a third-rate singer. The
manner in which Whitman has "translated," to use his modest expression, the song of the mocking-bird into words deserves boundless
admiration. I know of no other poem in which we find such a heart-
rending impersonation of a bird by a poet, such a welding of bird's
voice and human word, such an empathy for the joy and pain expressed by nature's singers. The European poets we have listed above
have accurately defined or admiringly praised the musical tone of the
bird-notes issuing from tiny throats, but no one attempted to choose

just those human articulate words[5] which would correspond to birds'
song if these creatures had possessed the faculty of speech (Eichendorff had the bird sing in the first person, but it sang conventional
Romantic lines) : the simple, over and over repeated exclamations of
a helpless being haunted by pain, which, while monotonously repeating the same *oh!* or giving in to the automatism that is characteristic
of overwhelming emotion ("my love, my love"), call upon all elements to bring back the mate. Thus in one common purpose the
whole creation is united by the bird in the manner of Saint Francis,
but this time in a dirge that associates the creation ("Oh night,"—
"Low-hanging moon," "Land, land, land," "Oh rising stars," "Oh
darkness") with the mourner, with his elemental body and his elemental desires "Oh throat," . . . "Oh throbbing heart," . . . "Oh past,"
"Oh happy life," "O songs of joy."[6] The mournful bird shakes out
"reckless de- /243/ spairing carols," songs of *world disharmony* in
which love and death are felt as irreconcilable enemies ("carols of
lonesome love,"—"death's carols"). The long outdrawn refrains of
despair ("soothe soothe soothe," "land land land," "loved loved
loved . . .") alternate with everyday speech whose minimum of ex-
pressivity becomes a maximum in a moment of tribulation that is
beyond words ("so faint, I must be still, be still to listen, but not
altogether still, for then she might not come immediately to me," or
"O darkness, O in vain! O I am very sick and sorrowful"). The most
dynamic American poet has here become the gentlest. We remember
Musset's lines quoted above; Whitman's bird's song is a *pur sanglot*.

We may surmise that this lyric section (within a lyric poem) has
been somewhat influenced by Mathew Arnold's "Forsaken Merman,"
("Come dear children, let us away, down and always below. / Come
dear children, come away down, call no more . . ."). But Arnold's
merman is one of the last offsprings of that futile masquerade of
elementary spirits revived by the Romantics, a pagan demon who is
presented as *defeated* by Christianity instead of a figure dangerously
seductive to Christians. But Whitman's mocking-bird, the spirit become human, who symbolizes all earthly loveliness subject to grief
and death, will live forever. It is one of those historical miracles we
can not explain that in the age of machines and capitalism there
should arise a poet who feels himself to be a brother to nature as
naturally as did Saint Francis, but who at the same time was enough

---

[5] Onomatopoeas (for example *tweet-tweet*) such as occur in folk-poetry would
be stylized phonetic approximations, neither human nor bird-like, of the inarticu-
late sounds of the birds.

[6] On this point, cf, Hermann Pongs. *Das Bild in der Dichtung* I, pp. 223 seq.

of an intellectual to know the uniqueness of his gift. To *him* the bird poured forth the "meanings which I of all men know, Yes my brother I know, the rest might not." This is again no boasting; this is the simple truth, a perspicacious self-definition of one who has a primeval genius of empathy for nature.

Now let us turn to the last part of the poem which begins with the words "demon *or* bird" (143), an expression followed later (175) by my "dusky demon *and* brother." The Shellyean ambiguity disappears here. This marks the end of the parabola that began with "the two feathered guests from Alabama" (26) and was continued sadly with "the solitary guest from Alabama" (51) and "the lone singer wonderful" (58). While the mood of the birds develops from careless rapture to 'dusky' /244/ melancholy, a contrary change takes place in the sea. "The fierce old mother incessantly mourning" (134), the "savage old mother incessantly crying" (141) becomes the "old crone rocking the cradle,"[7] "hissing melodious," "laving me all over." The two opposite developments must be seen in connection. To the degree that the bird is crushed by fate, the sea develops its soothing qualities; to the degree that beauty fades away, wisdom becomes manifest. The sea represents the sweet wisdom of death. The forces of nature are thus ambivalent, Janus-like. Nature wills sorrow and joy, life and death, and it may be that death will become or foster life. "Out of the cradle endlessly rocking," that is (we understand it now), out of the cradle of *death*, the poet will sing life. By presenting, in the beginning, the sea only as a cradle gently rocking, there was suggested the idea of birth and life; but now, the gently rocking cradle is seen as the symbol of recurring death and re-birth. A poet is born by the death of the bird who is a brother and a demon. A brother because he teaches the boy love; a demon, because he "projects"[8] the poet, anticipates, and

---

[7] Professor Anderson has drawn my attention to the fact that the parenthetic mention of the "old crone" is not contained in the first versions of the poem. In fact, the whole inversely parallel development of the bird and the sea is missing in them: 'Shelleyan' expression *demon or bird!* occurs only from 1867 on, the 1860 edition having only *bird!* in the passage in question, although this is followed by two allusions to (*dusky*) *demon*. Similarly the expression "dusky demon and brother" appears in final form only after several rewordings and owes its form to a meticulous carefulness on the part of that supposedly rather careless stylist Whitman, comparable indeed to that of the French classicist Malherbe who changed his first draft: "Et ne pouvait Rosette être mieux que les roses qui ne vivent qu'un jour" into the exquisite lines: "Rose, elle a vécu ce que vivent les roses, L'espace d'un matin" (cf. my *Stilstudien* II [1928], p. 18).

[8] This term must be understood in the light of what Christian theologians call 'prefiguration' or 'adumbration' (e.g. David, by his existence, announces or anticipates Christ who will be the *final king*). The bird in its song of grief attempts

heralds him, stirs up in him those creative faculties which must partake of the frightening and of the daemoniac. But while the bird was destined to teach the boy love ("death" being a reality the bird was not able to reconcile with love), the sea, wiser than the bird and the "aroused child's heart," has another message to bring to the boy: "Death, death, death, death, death" (173). This line is /245/ the counterpart of the mocking-bird's "loved loved loved loved loved!", and it is couched in the same exclamational style, as though it were the organic continuation thereof. The word *death* is "the word final, superior to all," "the key," "the clew" which awakes in the boy the thousand responses, songs, echoes, and the myriad of words; and once he has discovered this *meaning* of life, which is death, he is no longer the boy of the beginning ("never again leave me to be the peaceful boy I was before"). He has become the poet, the "uniter[9] of here and hereafter," able to fuse the voices of the *musica mundana* into one symphony, and we the readers can now understand his words in their full depth. In the conclusion we recognize certain lines of the proem textually repeated but now clarified and deepened by the keyword; we understand at last the the symphonic[10] value of "that strong and delicious word" alluded to in the proem. The liquid fusion suggested by the sea of death is symbolized by the fluid syntax of the last three stanzas; the relative constructions which we find in l. 163

---

to unite the whole universe and thereby anticipates the poet who, having absorbed the teaching of the sea (he is not land-bound like the bird), will be able *truly* to 'unite' the cosmos in his poem.

[9] The "will to unite" in Whitman is reflected by his habit of leaping from the particular to a comprehensive *all* as in "the word of the sweetest songs, and all songs" or in a discarded version of our poem: "O how joys, dreads, convolutions, human shapes, and all shapes, spring as from graves around me!" One feels here the impatience of the 'uniter.'

[10] It must be noted that the "symphonic fusion" in our poem was achieved by Whitman only in the process of time (cf. also note 7): The title of the poem in the first versions, 1860 and 1867, was "A Word Out of the Sea"; the oracular word *Death!* appeared in two passages, repeated five times in each, and the climactic line: 'the word final, superior to all' was preceded by a passage of six lines, in which was repeated several times the exclamation: "oh, a word!" The original versions show then the orchestra of the world concert dominated by the monody of the oracle; the fierce old mother "out of" whom 'the word' was to come, was in the exalted position of the Delphian Pythia. It may be added that Whitman showed himself then also more conscious of the new "chaos" opening up before him as a consequence of his new awareness of his destination: "O a word! O what is my destination? (I fear it is henceforth chaos)." This line is deleted in the final draught, because it would have jarred with the role of the 'uniter' assumed by Whitman in the beginning, but its original presence confirms our view that the poet has felt it indeed to be his task to create cosmos out of chaos.

"Whereto answering the sea . . ." and l. 174 "Which I do not forget" weld the three stanzas together into one stream or chain which comprehends the question of the boy, the answer of the sea and his choice of avocation, into one melody in which inspiration flows uninterruptedly from the watery element to the poet. The /246/ bird and the poet have been given their respective solos in the symphony. The bird's solo is the *aria* and the boy's the *trio* of ears, soul, and tears; the endless counterpoint and contrabasso of the sea has accompanied their detached musical pieces. Now all voices blend in an *"unendliche Melodie,"* an infinite melody, the unfixed form of nineteenth-century pantheism, with Wagnerian orchestration. "But fuse the song of my dusky demon and brother . . . with the thousand responsive songs, at random, my own songs . . . and with them the key, the word up from the waves." The last word in the poem, however, is the personal pronoun *me*. Though placed inconspicuously in an unstressed position in the short line "the sea whispered to me," this personal word nevertheless represents a modest climax. It is to Whitman that has been revealed the musical meaning of the world, the chord formed by Eros and Thantos, the infinite cosmos created from infinite chaos, and, finally, his own microcosmic rôle in the creation. It is the knowledge of death that will make him the poet of life, of this world, *not* of the Hereafter. The promise in the beginning to sing of the Here and Hereafter can be said to have been fulfilled only if the Hereafter is understood as comprised in the Here.[11] We will note that no reference is made in Whitman's poem to the world harmony of the Christian Beyond in the manner of Milton. The fullness of life of which Whitman sings can come to an end only in the sealike, endlessly rocking embrace of nothingness, an end that is sweet and sensuous ("delicious" is Whitman's epithet), and, indeed, he appears sensuously to enjoy the sound of the word *death* that he so often repeats. We may pause at this point to remember that in 1860, one year after our lyric was written, Whitman gives expression to the same feeling in the poem "Scented herbage of my breast":

> You [the leaves] make me think of death,
> Death is beautiful from you (what indeed is finally
>   beautiful except death and love?)
> Oh I think it is not for life I am chanting here
>   my chant of lovers,

---

[11] Cf. the line in "Walt Whitman," 48: "No array of terms can say how much I am at peace about God, and about death?"

I think it must be for death . . . /247/
Death or life I am then indifferent, my soul declines to prefer
(I am not sure but the high soul of lovers welcomes death most).

The same feeling for the voluptuousness of death and the deathlike
quality of love we find not only in Wagner's *Tristan und Isolde*
(1857), in which we hear the same words applied to the love-scene
and to the death-scene, *unbewusst—höchste (Liebes-) Lust.* There is
also the same motif in Baudelaire's *Invitation* of 1857, in which the
'invitation' is the lure of death, described as voluptuous hashish and
scented lotus. Perhaps powerful personalities crave death as a libera-
tion from the burden of their own individuality, and sensuous poets
wish to have a sensuous death. Perhaps also the concurrence in one
motif of three poets not in direct contact with each other means that
their subtle sensitivity instinctively anticipated the death-germs im-
planted in a luxuriant, sensuous, worldly civilization of "Enrichissez-
vous," of Victorianism, and the Second Empire. This was long before
the *fin de siècle* generation of D'Annunzio, Barrès, Hofmannsthal and
Thomas Mann, when the theme of love-death, inherited from Baudelaire and Wagner, finally became the theme *par excellence.* But Whitman, unlike his two sickly European contemporary confrères will
remain for us not the poet of death (although the idea of death may
have perturbed him more than once), but the unique poet of American *optimism* and love of life, who has been able, naturally and na-
ively, to unite what in other contemporary poets tends to fall apart,
the life of man and that of nature.[12]

A last question arises. To what sub-genre does our lyrical poem
belong? It is obviously an *ode,* the genre made famous by Pindar,
Horace, Milton, and Hölderlin, if the ode may be defined as a solemn,
lengthy, lyric-epic poem that celebrates an event significant for the
community, such as, with Pindar, the victory of a champion in the
Olympic games. Ancient poems belonging to this very aristocratic
genre are filled with erudite mythological allusions since the origin
of the heroes must be traced back to gods or demigods. These odes are
also written /248/ in a difficult language that can not easily be sung,
for they are replete with whimsical breaks and changes of rhythm and
tone that reflect the fragmentary nature of the inspiration of the poet,
carried away as he is by his divine enthusiasm or θεία μανία. Of course,
as is true of all ancient poetry, the ode had no rhymes. In the period

---

[12] . . . And in addition to all that—though this peculiarity is not represented
in our poem—the vitality of the machine.

of the Renaissance this ancient genre was revived, but enjoyed only a precarious existence in modern literatures because the social set-up of Pindar's Greece was missing in our civilization, filled as it is with social resentment, and because the travesty involved in presenting contemporary figures as ancient heroes could be sadly disappointing. The genre fared relatively better in Germanic than in Romance literatures because the Romance languages are not free enough in word-formation to offer coinages worthy of Pindar and because Romance needs the rhyme as a constitutive element of verse. Ronsard's Pindaric odes were signal failures. Whitman has acclimated the ode on American soil and democratized it. The lyric-epic texture, the solemn basic tone and the stylistic variation, the whimsical word-coinages and the chaotic fragmentariness are preserved. The latter feature has even found a modern justification in the complexity of the modern world. For the rhymeless Greek verse, Whitman by a bold intuition found an equivalent in the Bible verset, but he used this meter in order to express a creed diametrically opposed to that of the Bible. Theoretically, he could have borrowed expressions of his pantheistic beliefs from the mythology of the Greeks, but in reality, he did away with *all* mythology, pagan as well as Christian. He replaces the pagan Pantheon by the deified eternal forces of nature to which any American of today may feel close. The Ocean is the old savage mother, not Neptune with the trident (a mother, a primeval chthonic goddess) and the bird is not Philomela, but the mocking-bird who is a demon of fertility (only in the phrase "feathered guests of Alabama" do we find a faint reminiscence of Homeric expression, the *epitheton constans*).[13] The Neo-Catholic poet Paul Claudel /249/ who, as recently as the last decades, gave the French for the first time a true ode and was able to do so only by a detour through America, by imitating Whitman (even the metric form of his free verse), found it necessary to discard Whitman's pantheistic naturalism and to replace it by the *merveilleux chrétien* which a hundred years ago Chateau-

---

[13] It may be noted that even this is no pure case of an 'epitheton constans' since it does not reappear in later situations; on the contrary, as we have said, the gay epithet 'feather'd guests from Alabama' will lead us to the melancholy 'loneful singer wonderful.' In the case of 'the savage old mother incessantly crying' there is from the start no indication of 'constancy' of attribution; *crying* is not an attribute, but a predicate. But that Whitman had the Homeric epithet in mind is shown by the line quoted above from 'Song to myself': 'Walt Whitman . . . of Manhattan the son' which is a travesty of the ancient type 'Ajax the Telamonian son.'

briand had introduced into French prose.[14] But it can not be denied that Whitman's ode can reach a wider range of modern readers than can Claudel's orthodox Catholic *grande ode.* As for the solemn event significant for the community which the ode must by its nature celebrate—this we have in the consecration of Walt Whitman as a poet, the glorification, not of a Greek aristocratic athlete born of Gods, but of a nameless American boy, a solitary listener and singer on a little-known Long Island shore who, having met with nature and with his own heart, becomes the American national poet, the democratic and priestly *vates Americanus.*

---

[14] Cf. my interpretation of an ode by Paul Claudel in *Linguistics and Literary History* (Princeton 1948, pp. 193 *seq.*). This ode, one of five intended "pour saluer le siècle nouveau," and reminiscent of Horace's *Carmen saeculare,* also glorifies the achievements of modern industry and in this manner replaces the *fin de siècle* pessimism of the poetic schools that preceded Claudel by a "siècle nouveau" optimism which harks back to Whitman.

Robert D. Faner

Recitative-Aria Structure in "Out of the Cradle"*

. . .

In two of his greatest poems, technically perhaps the most perfect of all, "Out of the Cradle Endlessly Rocking" and "When Lilacs Last in the Dooryard Bloom'd," Whitman employed the /174/ recitative-aria structure with consummate skill. In these poems perhaps more than in any others, even the non-musical reader can clearly detect Whitman's own distinction between the styles. The first of the two, which was the occasion for the author's comment that all of his poems were constructed in the manner of the Italian opera, was once described by him, anonymously, as a "curious warble." He went on to say, "The purport of this wild and plaintive song, well-enveloped, and eluding definition, is positive and unquestionable, like the effect of music. The piece will bear reading many times—perhaps, indeed, only comes forth, as from recesses, by many repetitions."

In the poem a boy, whom the poet identifies as himself, wanders to the seashore on a romantic night and hears a remarkable bird song. He absorbs it and *translates* it, the translation becoming a central part of the poem. To distinguish it from the descriptive and narrative introduction, it is cast in the form of an aria, and this time, so that there can be no confusing the two styles, it is printed in italics.

All of the aria's characteristics which have previously been noted are exemplified in the bird song in perfect form. Look at the opening lines:

---

* Reprinted from *Walt Whitman and Opera* (Philadelphia: University of Pennsylvania Press, 1951), pp. 173–77, by permission. Title supplied by editor.

Shine! shine! shine!
Pour down your warmth great sun!
While we bask, we two together,

Two together!

The first line here is especially impressive. Here are three identical sounds, and nothing more, making up a line. The voice must add beauty and richness to them. An opera composer, Bellini, for example, would have been able to put down in notes exactly what he wanted the voice to do by way of enriching the sounds, as he did in the opening phrases of the great aria, "Casta Diva." Whitman trusted to the instincts of his reader not to hurry the line, to enhance it as only the sound of the human voice could do. It is of more than a little interest to discover in this connection that the line, and all the others exactly like it in form throughout the aria, consisted of only two syllables when the work originally appeared in 1859. In 1867 the poet added the third repetition of the word, partly to bring it closer to the actual phrase of the bird and probably also as a concession to the fact that most hasty readers failed to prolong the tone sufficiently for the effect he wanted. Furthermore, the addition of another word permits a more interesting tonal pattern for the phrase. With two words, the reader has few possibilities for pitch variation; he may rise on the first and descend on the second, or rise on both or descend on both. With the addition of the third word the possibilities are numerous, the most logical being sustained notes, low on the first, high on the second, and intermediate on the third. This reading gives a rise and fall pattern of charm and variety. The fact of these alterations shows unquestionably that Whitman was by no means a careless, insensitive workman, but rather a craftsman with the same kind of interest in his work that a musician must have.

As the boy in the poem returns to the seashore he hears the love song of the bird change to a song first of waiting, then of overwhelming sorrow, as one of the birds fails to return. The tragic aria is longer than the initial one, but except for the minor key and the material of grief it is constructed exactly like the former; it is still the translation of the bird's song. Again the aria is introduced:

Listen'd to keep, to sing, now translating the notes,
Following you my brother.

Again there is the three-note phrase woven through it like the opening subject in an opera aria:

> *Soothe! soothe! soothe!*
> *Loud! loud! loud!*

But there is an artistic variation in the third occurrence:

> *Land! land! O land!*

And in the last occurrence a still greater variation occurs:

> *O past! O happy life! O songs of joy!*

Incidentally this line originally read simply "O past! O joy!" The present version, except for the word "happy," added in 1881, was prepared in 1867. The addition of the third exclamation shows /176/ that the poet thought of the line as a part of the repeated pattern, giving pleasure in its repetitions like subjects in a melody. What is really only a further variation of the same device of the reiterated note occurs in the last line of the aria but two, when the word *loved* is repeated not three but five times. Here is the final paroxysm of grief, the final and ultimate cry of despair.

Whitman may have found a hint as to the effectiveness of this repeated note in the operas of Rossini and Verdi, for as the latter's biographer, Toye, pointed out, one of Verdi's favorite methods for expressing strong emotion was the repetition of a single note, a trick which he copied from Rossini's opera *Aureliano in Palmira*. He may also have got the idea from Tennyson, of whom he once wrote: "To me, Tennyson shows more than any poet I know (perhaps has been a warning to me) how much is in the finest verbalism. There is such a latent charm in mere words, cunning collections, and in the voice ringing them, which he has caught and brought out, beyond all others—as in the line,

> And hollow, hollow, hollow, all delight."

Tennyson's lyric "Break, Break, Break" had been published in 1842, seventeen years before "Out of the Cradle."

Reiteration of a different sort is also to be found in the aria, achieving effects appropriate to poetry but possibly derived from music. For example, at the ends of sections of the aria, phrases are repeated:

> *But my love soothes not me, not me . . .*
> *It is lagging—O think it is heavy with love, with love . . .*

> *O madly the sea pushes upon the land,*
> *With love, with love ...*
>
> *Surely you must know who is here, is here. ...*

The repetitions, added in 1867 when Whitman apparently studied anew the musical qualities of the aria, have the effect of echo or antiphon, and give a wailing, haunting quality to the lines. The repetitions also serve to tie together the passages which they close, of course. The two arias, one joyfully caroling love and the other intoning tragedy, are also bound together, though separated by many lines of recitative, by the repetition of a phrase just as pas- /177/ sages of music are bound together by the repetition of a figure or theme. Closing the first aria:

> *While we two keep together.*

Closing the second:

> *We two together no more.*

If there were any doubt in the reader's mind as to the poet's artistic intentions in this poem, it is dispelled by the short line at the close of the lyric:

> The aria sinking. ...

The poem goes on to a close with a recitative explaining the significance of the aria to Whitman, a passage of great importance in understanding his work.

So, in a sense, does "Out of the Cradle" emerge as a kind of 'opera without music,' composed of recitatives and arias in the Italian style, and, like the operas it was fashioned after, telling its tragic story of love, separation, and death.

Gay Wilson Allen and Charles T. Davis

A Critical Note on
"Out of the Cradle"*

The three titles Whitman assigned this poem (see headnote) indicate that he himself debated its meaning. Was it simply "A Child's
Reminiscence"? Or more symbolically, "A Word out of the Sea"?
Not until the poet had improved the rhythm of the first line, making
it undulate like the motion of the waves, did his first line become a
/165/ good title. The word "Death" whispered by the sea means
essentially the same as the "key ... word" emerging out of the endless
rocking of the "cradle," except that "cradle" is itself highly suggestive, not only of motion, but of life—young life and, hence, birth.
Note the cycle already implied: cradle-death-birth.

The rhythm of the prologue (ll. 1–22) is marvelously appropriate.
Basically it is "falling rhythm"; *i.e.*, dactyllic and trochaic.

Oút of the | crádle | éndlessly | rócking,
Oút of the | mócking-bìrd's | thróat, the | músical | shúttle,

. . . .

Úp from the | mýstic | pláy of | shádows | twíning and | twísting as |
if thèy were a | líve,

Because many of the lines begin with a dactyl, this meter gives the
impression of dominating. And many other poets have used dactyllic
meter for sea poems, including Homer. But here Whitman also uses
syntax in a highly connotative manner: the long, undulating sentence,
with the subject not stated until line 20, and the predicate and object

---

* Reprinted by permission of the publisher from *Walt Whitman's Poems*, edited
by Gay Wilson Allen and Charles T. Davis, pp. 164–67. © 1955 by New York
University.

in 22—actually object and then predicate as the final word. This sentence gives the sensation of continued motion—up and down, in and out through shadows and briars—and literally the boy does walk on uneven ground in the deceptive moonlight down to the waves perpetually "rocking" the shore.

The poignant song of the bird, the ominous appearance of the moon, and the "fitful risings and fallings" of the ocean (the rhythm of the prologue) blend into a chaos of sense-stimuli, provoking and suggesting some great secret of life. Out of this chaos emerges a unity, aesthetically and philosophically, which the boy finally understands and, in understanding, is transported into manhood—and poethood. This is the real theme of the poem: how the boy became a man and a poet.

Is the poem based on a "real" experience? The aesthetic value of the poem does not rest on the answer to this question, but since it is so often raised, let us consider it. One of Whitman's personal friends remembered that he read this poem to her family, in 1858, as accurately as she could recall, and he had said it "was founded on a real incident."—R. M. Bucke, *Walt Whitman* (Philadelphia, 1883), p. 29. /166/ Many critics and biographers have assumed that the poem is an elegy, that someone whom the poet loved had died and this is his allegorical treatment of the occurrence. But "real incident" need not refer to anything more than the conduct of the mockingbird which supposedly had lost its mate. It is not unlikely that this much Whitman observed in his boyhood, when, according to ornithologists, there were mockingbirds on Long Island. That the song the boy heard was actually a lament was, of course, a subjective interpretation, either at the time or in retrospect. Sooner or later in life everyone has to face the stern fact of death in the natural order of things. Whether fact or fiction, the death of the female mockingbird is a good symbol of this fact in nature.

The story proper begins with line 23, told almost like a fairy tale, with simple imagery, past time ("Once [on] Paumanok"), and repetitive phraseology ("and ... and ..."). The song of the bird is later (1. 130) called an "aria," which is an elaborate melody sung to instrumental accompaniment in operas or cantatas. Attending the Italian opera was one of Whitman's greatest enjoyments, and here he is trying to construct a song on the analogy of the operatic "aria." He makes no attempt to imitate the trills, runs, or liquid notes of an actual bird song. In fact, anyone who has heard a mockingbird or a brown thrasher will find it difficult to imagine this song coming from the throat of a bird. But, then, neither does a bird use words!

This is what the poet (recalling a stage of his boyhood experience) imagines the bird to sing, to the accompaniment of the muted ocean music.

This poem is obviously highly subjective—though precisely how much of the story was literally true we do not know, and never can know. But the poet says the "solitary singer" projects him. The "cries of unsatisfied love" will henceforth never be absent from him. This must be the mature poet looking back over his past life; a boy would scarcely have these anticipations of such a fate in store for him. But when he begs for a "clew," he is putting himself back in the time when he, and by extension every human being, sought an answer to the meaning of suffering and death in the natural world. The bird, symbol of nature on the sensory level, does not give the answer; it comes from the sea, the "old crone rocking her cradle." The sea, therefore symbolizes the principle of maternity, which is to say birth and life. She whispers "death," but coming from the /167/ rocker of the "cradle," the implication is that death is but a natural transition to rebirth. The poem ends, therefore, on the note of im-, plied hope and faith to be found in every great cultural myth and world religion. The calm, softness, brevity, and simplicity of the final line imply complete emotional resignation and intellectual acceptance.

Clark Griffith

From Sex and Death: The Significance of Whitman's *Calamus* Themes

. . .

Any number of 1860 poems reflect and extend the mood of *Calamus*. There is "So Long!", for instance, which echoes the note of finality in "Long I thought." Or in "As I Ebb'd with the Ocean of Life," one finds the same dark unbeliefs which characterize "Terrible Doubt of Appearances." Or Whitman's obsession with death could be traced through a large group of 1860 compositions, particularly through a cluster that was never afterward reprinted. Each of these other poems shares this in common with *Calamus*, however: that it expresses some strange new outlook of Whitman's, yet provides, within its own context, no clue concerning the way in which the outlook developed. To comprehend /31/ the ambiguities, one must examine them against the backdrop of Whitman's 1855 and 1856 material, then try to re-construct what lay between.

But what of "Out of the Cradle Endlessly Rocking," published separately by Whitman in 1859 as "A Child's Reminiscence," and then immediately re-introduced into the 1860 edition?[1] Here, surely, is a poem in which an act of psychological change *is* dramatized, the shift from one point of view into quite another *does* constitute a central situation. In its narrative form and elegiac tone, further-more, "A Child's Reminiscence" is markedly different from any-thing Whitman had written previously. Is it possible, then, that

---

* Reprinted from *Philogical Quarterly*, xxxix (January, 1960), 30–37, by per-mission of the publisher, The University of Iowa.
[1] "A Child's Reminiscence" first appeared in *The New York Saturday Press*, December 24, 1859. Re-titled "A Word out of the Sea," it was printed in the 1860 edition.

the poem somehow prefigures *Calamus*? The discovery on the beach
and the transition from "childhood" to "maturity" which the discovery motivates: are these perhaps Whitman's symbolic account of
the realizations which underlay *Calamus*, making *Calamus* both
possible and deeply tragic?

Using the text of the original version, let us see what can be made
of the narrative portions of "A Child's Reminiscence." When the
poem opens, the discovery it will recount is already an accomplished
fact. The time is the present; the figure in the foreground is one
whom we might designate as the "mature poet"; and the "mature
poet's" surroundings are symbolic, presumably, of the anguish that a
new insight has taught. It is therefore worth taking careful stock of
the details from which this introductory scene has been fabricated.
Death broods everywhere, unnamed as yet, but persistently implied by
the mysterious, unspoken "word" and the ominous rustlings of the
sea. Complementing death is a general sense of sterility, conveyed
through the "sterile sands" of the beach, the references to "briars"
and "driftings" and Autumn midnight. The gloom and "mystic play
of shadows" seem as much psychological symbols as parts of the
seascape; for both alike body forth the "poet's" despondency and
objectify his loneliness. Clearly, no comparable set of images had
existed in Whitman's poetry of 1855 and 1856. Between this dis-
quieting scene and even the most introspective passages in "Song of
Myself," there stretches a uniquely different conception of things;
and the emphasis here upon death, decay, and sickness looks not
backward, but ahead—ahead to the *Calamus* poetry already being
composed. But /32/ having struck notes that would resound fre-
quently in *Calamus*, Whitman promptly broaches the subject that
Calamus would never directly mention. Not only is a profoundly
altered outlook to appear in "A Child's Reminiscence"; the causes of
the alteration are likewise to be set forth. In memory, the "mature
poet" will return to his "childhood" (or former self) and to a trans-
forming experience that happened in his past. By re-creating this
episode, he can account for why, in the present moment, his songs are
framed by a death-haunted beach.

Coming in the wake of so solemn a beginning, the first part of the
reminiscence achieves a surprisingly jubilant air. The "child" is the
observer now, but a "child" endowed with full poetic powers evidently, since his responses are the distinctively creative responses of
"peering, absorbing, translating." And the scene that reflects the
"child's" viewpoint is not simply different from the opening tableau;
in every important respect, the components are exact opposites of
those in the prelude. Images of death and deprivation give way, for

example, to metaphors suggesting love, happiness and life. All these qualities are embodied in the two birds, who symbolize love and the perfect love-union obviously, but who are also cast as fertility symbols, through allusions to the "light green eggs" and the "she-bird crouched on her nest." In addition, the power of love is indicated by the recurring phrase "two together," a phrase that is used twice in the description of the birds and three times more in the lyric which the birds are heard to sing. Finally, it is apparent that Nature is now divested of the sinister aspects which prevailed at the outset. As before, the scene is the beach, but a sun-drenched beach this time, and one where Autumn midnight has been supplanted by Spring and Summer. Nature is beneficent, compassionate, a life-giving force; when the birds sing, they eulogize natural objects, make Nature an ecstatic partner in their own shared ecstasy. From dirge-like beginnings, in short, "A Child's Reminiscence" has passed over into a rhapsodic idyll. And what crowd through the child's imagination are a host of familiar shapes from Whitman's heterosexual love poetry: the same "pairing of birds" that took place in "From Pent-up Aching Rivers," for instance, or the "Earth of Love" apostrophized in "Spontaneous Me," or the same "he-bird" and "she-bird" that symbolized the miracle of life in an 1856 "fertility" poem called "This Compost."

But in "A Child's Reminiscence" the idyll comes to an end. /33/ Suddenly the "she-bird crouched not on the nest." Possibly she has been killed; in any case the significant fact is that she never "appeared again." And hard upon her disappearance, the memory takes a gloomier turn, as the night imagery of the prelude is re-evoked and within the "child's" consciousness there break out the refrains of the "he-bird," warbling his grief from the "prong of a moss-scallop'd stake." At this point, the crucial center in the drama of discovery has been reached. Whatever the "child" is to learn—whatever psychological change it is that will transform him from "child-hood" to "poethood" (or cause him to forsake one kind of poetic vision for another)—the essence of the new truth is conveyed symbolically through the male bird's aria: that point is reiterated constantly as the poem proceeds. It is essential, therefore, to see in the aria a statement of the "child's" growing comprehension of himself, and to read it not only for what it may seem to say, but also for meanings or relationships that are perhaps established below the surface.

And there is, in fact, a certain ambiguity about the song. Ostensibly it represents an impassioned lament for the loss of "two together." As the lament develops, however, one finds that this

particular loss shades off into a bereavement that is more generalized, more fundamental. For with a curious insistence, the singer
is made to pair the loss of the female with a larger and deeper
privation: with the sense of alienation which he himself now experiences when he contemplates natural objects. Gradually it becomes apparent that the real source of the grief he chants is less the
loss of "two together" than a (perhaps consequent) loss of status in
the world of Nature.

Thus the song begins with a series of pathetic fallacies, especially
intriguing because the first and last are close paraphrases of lines
that initially appeared in Whitman's poetry on heterosexual love:[2]

> *Soothe! Soothe!*
> *Close on its wave soothes the wave behind,*
> *And again another behind, embracing and lapping, every one close,*
> *But my love soothes not me.*
>
> *Low hangs the moon—it rose late,*
> *O it is lagging—O I think it is heavy with love.*
>
> *O madly the sea pushes upon the land*
> *With love—with love.*

The import is clear enough. All natural phenomena are merged /34/
through love; as in the heterosexual poetry, it is the rhythm of
passion which binds disparates like land and sea, earth and moon
into a felicitous totality. But for the singer, deprived of a female
counterpart, a place in this cohesive scheme no longer exists. Lacking
the love that soothes, he is, as the blunt, heavy antithesis in the
opening stanza indicates, a stranger in Nature, an exception to the
workings of the natural order. And the degree of this exclusion is
subtly enlarged when the singer goes on to appeal to Nature. With
verbal gestures meant to remind us of the duet of "two together," he
addresses himself to various natural objects, turning for pity and
comfort to the moon and land, the stars, the sea, the darkness. The
failure of each to respond re-enforces the idea of Nature's indiffer-
ence. Moreover, the behavior of particular phenomena, which are
portrayed as deluding the singer, as victimizing him with false appearances—this suggests that Nature has been invested with a quality
quite demonic, and that the cleavage between singer and his
surroundings is as deep as may be.

---

[2] Compare these details from "Pent-up Aching Rivers": ". . . of the pairing of
birds, . . . of the lapping of waves,/Of the mad pushes of waves upon the land—I
these chanting."

It is to deepen in still another way, however. For now as the aria mounts toward a climax, a weird and ambiguous spectacle occurs which seals irrevocably the connection between the female's disappearance and a tragic alteration on the face of Nature. Even as the singer invokes compassion from the world about him, the image of the female is everywhere superimposed across natural phenomena, and superimposed in such a fashion that Nature itself seems shorn of power, on the verge of depletion and imminent collapse. The symbol of loss is thus generalized into a shadow on the land, a "troubled reflection" in the sea; it is made a dusky blemish on the "waning, drooping" moon, a star that fails to rise, a dark shape among the "fluttering" breakers. In contradistinction, then, to the vibrant world containing "two together," Nature has become a mirror of woe, the source of terrible and morbid appearances. The burden of the "child's" discovery would seem to be that, with the female gone, Nature assumes a guise that is both forbidding and sepulchral. And reading backward, we begin to have some inkling of why, at the outset, it was a grim and death-like scene which bespoke the agitations of the "mature poet."

But what can be gleaned from the narrative as a whole? Something; a good deal perhaps; enough at least to warrant reconsideration of three salient features, each of which may, in turn, give rise to a hypothesis. /35/

We have seen, first of all, that the idyll of "two together" reads like a compressed version of Whitman's earlier love poetry. The bird symbols are identical. There is a similar association of love with life and with the perpetual rebirth of Nature. Above all, the notion that "two together" lends itself to "absorption" and "translation," that it constitutes the stuff of which poetry can be made— this indicates a clear parallel to the kind of love poetry being composed by Whitman in 1855 and 1856. By 1859, however, his love poetry had broadened into a radically different vein—a point which may explain why, in "A Child's Reminiscence," the idyll belongs to the past, to the period before discovery, and is inaccessible to the "mature poet" except through an act of memory.

Whitman's new love poetry involved a glorification of manly attachments. That was the positive side of *Calamus*. On the other hand, despair and dismay also crept into the material; and in retrospect, these negative qualities seem attributable to one key circumstance: to what might properly be called Whitman's wilful destruction of woman. This is a bald way of stating the matter perhaps (though in point of fact the symbolic "slaying" of the female is often a

hidden theme in homosexual writing). But in Whitman's case there
is really no other way to state it. For unuttered and implicit though
it is, the significant omission from *Calamus* is the omission of
woman, the unrelenting exclusion of any conceivable grounds for
"two together." It is a point which may explain why, in "A Child's
Reminiscence," discovery commences with the "destruction" of the
she-bird and why her disappearance, though dramatized casually as
an event and even rather unfeelingly, nevertheless results in complex
problems for the singer who survives.

For to Whitman, precisely because he was Whitman, the destruction of the female had to be fraught with grave and ominous compli-
cations. As we have observed, Whitman identified femininity with
creativity. Though Woman might exist for him as a mere label, a
groundless concept, he could still exalt her as "exit of the rest"; he
could dramatize her as the source of life and regeneration on a
cosmic scale. To exclude her from his love poetry might become an
emotional necessity, therefore; but it was an exclusion that inevitably
gave rise to a terrifying process of self-exclusion. For by turning away
from heterosexual themes, Whitman found himself trapped in a
philosophical *cul-de-sac* from where, as it were, *rapprochements*
with the normal, love-created uni- /36/ verse were no longer possible:
from where he was at once an outcast in that universe and guilty of
thoughts which threatened it with annihilation. And these are points
which may explain why, in "A Child's Reminiscence," the "child,"
bereft of his vision of the female, hears his "demon" lament the
otherness of Nature, and is changed into the "mature poet," medi-
tating over a scene from which all signs of life seem to have been
systematically drained away.

But the test of these hypotheses lies, of course, in the reverie
which brings "A Child's Reminiscence" to a close. In this concluding movement, the transfigured "child" is made to offer his own
interpretation of what discovery has signified, and to trace out its
enduring effects upon his future destiny. Hence if Whitman has
written the poem out of a premonition of personal disaster—or if,
to use Mr. Kenneth Burke's terms, the shift from "childhood" to
"poethood" symbolically re-enacts Whitman's own shift from
heterosexual to homosexual poetry—it is here, more than anywhere
else, that this autobiographical element ought to emerge most
forcefully.

Observe, then, that the symbolic destruction of the female is to
make the "child" not only a "mature poet," but a writer of *love*

poetry as well. In time Whitman would wish to blur over this interesting fact and would delete a key phrase in order to conceal it. But in 1859–60, the "child" is not just the "outsetting bard" who appears in later versions of "Out of the Cradle Endlessly Rocking." He is, instead, an "outsetting bard of love."

Consider, next, the qualities with which his forthcoming love songs will be imbued. They are to be scored by a "sweet hell within," to resound with cries of unsatisfied passion. But in 1859–60 their nature is still more sharply defined in a half-dozen verses which Whitman would choose never to reprint. "O what is my destination?" cries the "child"; and this strange and dreadful prophecy ensues:

> O I fear it is henceforth chaos!
> O how joys, dreads, convolutions, human shapes and all shapes,
>   spring as from graves around me!
> O phantoms! You cover all the land and all the sea!
> O I cannot see in the dimness whether you smile or frown upon me!
> O vapor, a look, a word! O well-beloved!
> O you dear women's and men's phantoms!

So close are the lines to anticipating the essential spirit of *Calamus* that comment seems all but superfluous. One notes simply that if /37/ the new love poetry is to be utterly unlike Whitman's material of 1855 and 1856, what the poetry will contain are the same phantom shapes of "Of him I Love Day and Night," the yawning emptiness which will overspread "Terrible Doubt of Appearances," the same acute guilt feelings which are to pervade *Calamus* from begining to end.

Or consider, finally, how with *Calamus* in mind, the last cryptic scene in "A Child's Reminiscence" acquires greater clarity and meaningfulness. Death is the "word" which completes the "child's" tragic vision, and death is to be the condition Whitman beholds most insistently throughout *Calamus*. Furthermore, death is revealed to the "child" by the "savage old mother," rolled up to him, like an insidious secret, from the "liquid rims" of the sea. And recognizing the womb-figure here, we see that it symbolizes again the horrifying truth which Whitman glimpsed in sexual inversion—that the image stands, indeed, as the obverse side of the symbolism presented in "Scented Herbage of My Breast." For just as the phallus must be everlastingly sterile in a world of comrades, just so the womb must carry there connotations of infertility. What Whitman has banished from "A Child's Reminiscence" and will destroy again in *Calamus* is the basis upon which life renews itself. Accordingly, the "exit of the rest" can now emit only barrenness and death. Beyond much doubt, this last perception of the "child's" is the one which invests *Calamus* with its tragic colorations. And one feels that the distance from the "mature poet's" death-ridden songs to the songs of *Calamus* is the distance of only a step. . . .

Roy Harvey Pearce

From Whitman Justified: The Poet in 1860*

. . .

The central terms in the argument of the 1860 *Leaves of Grass,* I suggest, run something like this: first, in the poems which lead up to "A Word Out of the Sea"—self-discovery, self-love, rebirth, diffusion-of-self, art; and second, in the poems which follow "A Word Out of /287/ the Sea"—love-of-others, death, rebirth, reintegration-of-self, art, immortality. The sequence is that of an ordinary life, extra-ordinarily lived through; the claims are strictly humanistic. The child manages somehow to achieve adulthood; the movement is from a poetry of diffusion to a poetry of integration. Immortality is the *result* of art, not its origin, nor its cause. The humanism is painful, because one of its crucial elements (centering on "death" as a "clew" in "A Word out of the Sea") is an acknowledgment of all-too-human limitations and constraints. So long as Whitman lived with that acknowledgment, lived *in* that acknowledgment—even when living with it drove him (as it too often did) toward bathos and sentimental-ism—, he managed to be a poet, a "secretary," a "sage," a seer, a visionary. His religion was the religion of humanity: the only religion that a work of art can *directly* express, whatever other religion it may confront and acknowledge. *Indirectly,* it *can* confront religion in the more usual and more proper, sense; for it can treat of man in his aspiration for something beyond manhood, even if it cannot claim—since its materials are ineluctably those of manhood—to treat directly of that something-beyond. The burden—someone has called it the

---

* Reprinted from *The Minnesota Review,* I (1961), 286–291, by permission of the publishers and author. The essay appears in expanded form as the introduction to a facsimile edition of the 1860 *Leaves of Grass* (Cornell University Press, 1961).

burden of incertitude; Keats called it "negative capability"—is a
hard one to bear. Whitman, I am suggesting, bore it most successfully,
bore it most successfully for us, in the 1860 *Leaves of Grass.*

Which brings me to the most important of the poems first collected
in this volume, "A Word Out of the Sea." It was originally published
separately in 1859, as "A Child's Reminiscence." Thus far, I have tried
to suggest the proper context in which the poem should be read: as
part of the volume for which it was originally written; as a turning
point in the argument of that book. Note that "A Word Out of the
Sea" comes about mid-way in the book after "Walt Whitman," the
"Chants Democratic," "Leaves of Grass," "Salut au Monde," and
"Poem of Joys"—that is, after those poems which tell us of the poet's
discovery of his powers as poet and of his ability to use those powers
so to "vivify" his world, and himself in it: after his discovery that it
is man's special delight and his special agony to be at once the subject
and object of his meditations; after his discovery that consciousness
inevitably entails self-consciousness and a sense of the strengths and
weaknesses of self-consciousness. Moreover, "A Word Out of the Sea"
comes shortly before the "Enfans d'Adam" and "Calamus" sequences
/288/ —that is, shortly before those poems which work out the
dialectic of the subject-object relationship under the analogue of
the sexuality of man as creator of his world and of persons, places,
and things as its creatures. I cannot but think that Whitman knew
what he was doing when he placed "A Word Out of the Sea" thus.
For he was obligated, in all his autobiographical honesty, to treat
directly of man's fallibilities as well as his powers, to try to discover
the binding relationship between fallibilities and powers: to estimate
the capacity of man to be himself and the cost he would have to pay.
The poems which come before "A Word Out of the Sea" have little
to do with fallibilities; they develop the central terms of the whole
argument only this far: self-discovery, self-love, rebirth, art. Theirs
is the polymorph perverse world of the child. In them, death only
threatens, does not promise; power is what counts. The turning-point
in the poet's life can come only with the "adult" sense of love and
death, the beginning and the end of things: out of which issues art,
now a mode of immortality. In "A Word Out of the Sea" the 1860
volume has its turning-point. Beyond this poem, we must remember,
are the "Enfans d'Adam" and "Calamus" sequences, and also "Crossing Brooklyn Ferry" and the "Messenger Leaves" sequence.

The 1860 poem begins harshly: "Out of the rocked cradle." The
past participle, unlike the present participle in the later versions, implies no agent for the rocking; the sea here is too inclusive to be a

symbol; it is just a fact of life—life's factuality. Then comes the
melange of elements associated with the "sea." They are among the
realities whose miraculousness the poet is on his way to understanding. Note the third line (omitted in later versions) which clearly es-
tablishes the autobiographical tone and makes the boy at once the
product of nature at large and a particular nature: "Out of the boy's
mother's womb, from the nipples of her breasts." All this leads to a
clear split in point of view, so we know that the poet-as-adult is
making a poem which will be his means to understanding a childhood
experience. Initially we are told of the range of experiences out of
which this poem comes: the sea as rocked cradle seems at once literally (to the boy) and metaphorically (to the poet) to "contain" the
song of the bird, the boy's mother, the place, the time, the memory
of the brother, and the as yet unnamed "word stronger and more
delicious than any" which marks a limit to the meaning of the whole.
This is /289/ quite explicitly an introduction. For what follows is
given a separate title, "Reminiscence," as though the poet wanted
to make quite plain the division between his sense of himself as
child and as adult. Then we are presented with the story of the birds,
the loss of the beloved, and the song sung (as only *now* the poet
knows it) to objectify this loss, so make it bearable, so assure that it
can, in *this* life, be transcended. Always we are aware that the
poet-as-adult, the creative center of the poem, seeks that "word
stronger and more delicious" which will be his means finally to
understand his reminiscences and—in the context of this volume (I
emphasize: in the context of *this* volume)—serve to define his vocation as poet: at once powerful and fallible. The points of view of
bird, child, and adult are kept separate until the passage which
reads:

> Bird! (then said the boy's Soul,)
> Is it indeed toward your mate you sing? or is it mostly to me?
> For I that was a child, my tongue's use sleeping,
> Now that I have heard you,
> Now in a moment I know what I am for—I awake
> And already a thousand singers—a thousand songs, clearer
>   louder, more sorrowful than yours,
> A thousand warbling echoes have started to life within me,
> Never to die.

The boy, even as a man recalling his boyhood, does not, as in later
versions, at first address the bird as "Demon." He is at this stage in-

capable of that "or"—in the later reading "Demon or bird." Even
though his soul speaks, he is to discover—some lines later—his special "poetic" relation to the bird. Moreover, as "boy," he holds toward
death an attitude halfway between that of the bird—who is merely
"instructive" and that of the man—who is "reflective," capable of
"reminiscence." Yet the points of view begin to be hypnotically
merged—*after* the fact. In the boy's "soul" the poet discovers a child's
potentiality for adult knowledge; but he keeps it as a potentiality, and
he never assigns it to the bird, who (or which) is an occasion merely.
Yet having seen that potentiality as such, he can "now," in the adult
present, work toward its realization, confident that the one will follow
necessarily in due course from the other. Now, in the adult present,
he can ask for "the clew," "The word final, superior to all," the word
which "now" he can "conquer." I cannot emphasize too much that
/290/ it is a "word"—that the poet is translating the sea (and all it
embodies) as pre-linguistic fact into a word, knowledge of which will
signify his coming to maturity. "Out of," in the original title, is meant
quite literally to indicate a linguistic transformation. In the record of
the growth of his mind, he sees *now* that the word will once and for
all precipitate the meaning he has willed himself to create, and in the
creating to discover. And it comes as he recalls that time when the
sea, manifesting the rhythm of life and death itself,

> Delaying not, hurrying not,
> Whispered me through the night, and very plainly before daybreak,
> Lisp'd to me the low and delicious word DEATH,
> And again Death—ever Death, Death, Death. . . .

(Not "Death," merely repeated four times as in later versions—but
"ever," beyond counting. The prophetic Whitman was bound to drop
that "ever," since for him nothing was beyond counting.)

   The merging of the points of view occurs as not only past and present, child and adult, but subject and object (i.e., "The sea. . . whispered me"—not "*to* me") are fused. The poet now knows the word,
because he has contrived a situation in which he can control its use;
he has discovered (to recall the language of the *American Primer*
notes) another reality, one that words until *now* had not been formed
to represent. He has, as only a poet can, *made* a word out of the sea—
for the duration of the poem understood "sea" as it may be into
"Death"—"ever Death." His genius is such as to have enabled us to
put those quotation marks around the word—guided by him, to have
"bracketed" this portion of our experience with language; and we

discover that as language binds us in the poet's time, so it is bound in human time.

If the end of the poem is to understand cosmic process as a continual loss of the beloved through death and a consequent gain of death-in-life and life-in-death—if this is the end of the poem, nonetheless it is gained through a creative act, an assertion of life in the face of death, and a discovery and acknowledgment of the limits of such an assertion. And this act is that of the very person, the poet, whom death would deprive of all that is beloved in life. Moreover, the deprivation is quite literally that and shows the poet moving, in high honesty, from the "Enfans d'Adam" sequence to "Calamus." In the 1860 vol- /291/ ume, "A Word Out of the Sea" entails the "Calamus" sequence. (What if Whitman had, in "A Word Out of the Sea," written "comrade" instead of "brother"?)

In any case, at this stage of his career, Whitman would not yield to his longing for such comfort as would scant the facts of life and death. There is, I repeat, that opening "rocked," not "rocking" cradle; there is the quite naturalistic acknowledgement of the "boy's mother's womb." And there is stanza 31 (the stanzas in the 1860 poem are numbered, as the stanzas of the final version are not) :

> O give me some clew!
> O if I am to have so much, let me have more!
> O a word! O what is my destination?
> O I fear it is henceforth chaos!
> O how joys, dreads, convolutions, human shapes, and all
>   shapes, spring as from graves around me!
> O phantoms! you cover all the land, and all the sea!
> O I cannot see in the dimness whether you smile or frown
>   upon me;
> O vapor, a look, a word! O well-beloved!
> O you dear women's and men's phantoms!

In the final version, the equivalent stanza reads only:

> O give me the clew (it lurks in the night here somewhere,)
> O if I am to have so much, let me have more!

The difference between "some clew" and "the clew" marks the difference between a poet for whom questions are real and one for whom questions are rhetorical. The later Whitman was convinced that the lurking clew would find him—and to that degree, whatever else he was, was not a poet. The earlier Whitman, in all humility, feared that what might issue out of this experience was "phantoms"—a good enough word for aborted poems. And often—but not too often— he was right.

Finally, there is not in "A Word Out of the Sea" the falsely (and, in the context of the poem, undeservedly) comforting note of "Or like some old crone rocking the cradle, swathed in sweet garments, bending aside." Indeed, the sentimentality and bathos of this too-much celebrated line, as I think, is given away by the fact that it is the only simile, the only "like" clause, in the poem. And, in relation to the total effect of the poem, the strategic withdrawal of the "Or" which introduces the line is at least unfortunate, at most disastrous.

Emory Holloway

Lyric on Love and Death*

It must have been in September of this year that Whitman took
another giant step forward as an artist when he composed a masterful
lyric on love and death. He first read the manuscript at the home of
his close friend, Mrs. Abby Price, whom he told that the poem was
based on a real incident, as the original title, "A Child's Reminiscence," would suggest. As a barefoot boy wandering the Paumanok
shores at midnight, he had once come upon a nest of mockingbirds
singing in full-throated happiness in just being together, indifferent
to the external alternations of nature. But one day the she-bird fails
to return and is supposed to be dead. Her mate sings a broken-hearted
aria, appealing like an operatic tenor to the elements, the earth
spirit, the mocking waves and the shifting shadows. The poem story
concerns the effect that this miniature heartbreak has on the soul of
the impressionable boy-poet, who, for the first time guessing the
meaning of death, has learned from the bird-artist not only how to
coin life's tragedy /93/ into song but how to get behind appearances
and find in the universal order of things assurance that death is after
all a strong and "delicious" word.

> Bird! (then said the boy's soul,)
> Is it indeed toward your mate you sing? or is it mostly to me?
> For I that was a child, my tongue's use sleeping,
> Now that I have heard you,
> Now in a moment I know what I am for—I awake,

* Reprinted from *Free and Lonesome Heart: The Secret of Walt Whitman*
(New York: Vantage Press, 1960), pp. 92–94, by permission of the author. Title
supplied by editor.

83

And already a thousand singers—a thousand songs, clearer,
    louder, more sorrowful than yours,
A thousand warbling echoes have started to life within me,
Never to die.

Of course it is not necessary to assume that Whitman became the
tongue-freed poet when a boy, though in his young manhood he did
compose quite a number of melancholy poems on death; in fact, we
have seen that he did not. Nor are we warranted in assuming that the
beginning of his poetic career is traceable to an experience that
appears to have been recent at the time of writing "Out of the Cradle
Endlessly Rocking," to judge from its phrases of poignant sorrow.
We have seen him ten years earlier making that beginning. More
than once he senses the "terrible doubt of appearances," so that he
was forever seeking "the real Me" and the reality which has no
relation to time and its changes. When he finds his message of love
("the outsetting bard of love"), or when he finds a satisfying lover or
friend, he strikes through the masks of life and feels for the moment
secure. The word "death" used so dominantly in the poem need not
be taken literally, and some critics are inclined to interpret it as the
death of that self which makes parting such bitter pain, the reabsorp-
tion of the individual soul into the pantheistic All, the return of the
personal identity to the "float" whence it has been struck by bodily
contact with men and nature, as he had described in the Brooklyn
Ferry poem. Nevertheless the poem could hardly have been con-
ceived had the /94/ poet not somehow become "brother" to the
bereaved bird, just as in "When Lilacs Last in the Dooryard Bloom'd"
he becomes the thrush's alter ego; and to do this he must somewhere
have learned the suffering of personal loss. No one in his family had
died and we know of no particular friend recently lost to him. The
imagery of the allegory seems to indicate the loss of a female lover,
though some who lean toward the view that Whitman was homosexual in his emotional equipment think that about this time he
must have lost, or lost the affection of, some male comrade. But a
measure of the excellence of this widely admired poem is to be found
in the degree to which he is able to universalize the theme presented
and the musical harmony whereby he accepts the ordinances of
nature.

Stephen E. Whicher

Whitman's Awakening to Death*

Toward a Biographical Reading of "Out of the Cradle Endlessly Rocking"

There is no life in thee, now, except that rocking life imparted by a gently rolling ship; by her, borrowed from the sea; by the sea, from the inscrutable tides of God. But while this sleep, this dream is on ye, move your foot or hand an inch; slip your hold at all; and your identity comes back in horror. Over Descartian vortices you hover. And perhaps, at midday, in the fairest weather, with one half-throttled shriek you drop through that transparent air into the summer sea, no more to rise for ever. Heed it well, ye Pantheists!   *Moby-Dick*, "The Masthead."

It is still too little realized that, with the possible but not obvious exception of Melville, no American author has ever engaged in a more daring or eventful voyage of the mind than Whitman. In his later years Whitman himself for some reason attempted to hide its extent, retouched and toned down his most revealing poems and ingeniously fitted them together into a structure toward which he claimed he had been working all the time. This jerry-built monument to the aging Whitman, which remains to this day the basis of nearly all anthologies of his work and is still reverently toured by uncritical guides, is actually a major obstacle to the recognition of his true stature. Fortunately a strong critical tradition[1] has now for many years

* Reprinted from *Studies in Romanticism*, I (Autumn 1961), 9–27, by permission.
[1] See particularly Jean Catel, *Walt Whitman: la naissance du poète* (Paris, 1929); Frederik Schyberg, *Walt Whitman* (Copenhagen, 1933), trans. Evie Allison Allen (New York, 1951); and Roger Asselineau, *L'évolution de Walt Whitman après la première édition des Feuilles d'Herbe* (Paris, 1954), Part I trans. and rev. as *The Evolution of Walt Whitman: The Creation of a Personality* (Cambridge, Mass.,

/10/ been working to lay bare for us the real structure of Whitman's work, the spiritual biography that emerges from a comparative reading of all the editions of his *Leaves*. In this paper I wish to re-examine some part of this story as it emerges from certain key poems of the 1855 and 1860 editions, in particular "Out of the Cradle."[2]

For this purpose it is convenient to accept the periods, or phases, which Floyd Stovall distinguished nearly thirty years ago[3] and which time has only confirmed (the names are mine): Whitman's first or transcendental phase runs from 1855 through 1858; the second or tragic phase begins with 1859 and runs through the first publication of "When Lilacs Last" in 1865; the third or philosophic phase comprises the rest of his poetic career. This is the framework of the discussion that follows, which will center on the years 1855–60. In these years, I shall argue, it is not enough to say that a new note entered Whitman's work or that he passed through a time of serious trouble; the whole character of his work was radically and permanently altered. To trace this change in the space I have I will focus on one theme only, what Asselineau calls Whitman's obsession with death.[4]

A major theme of the poems of the first phase, of course, is the poet's victory over death. In every possible way these poems deny the finality of death and proclaim immortality. In this they make particularly plain what Schyberg has called Whitman's "optimism in defiance,"[5] for a preoccupation with death marks not merely the young Whitman's Emmeline Grangerford period but later apprentice work, too, and is evidenced in the early *Leaves* themselves in the very frequency with which his victory has to be re-enacted. The

---

1960). This paper starts from their essential conclusions and attempts to take a further step. In particular, it accepts without argument Schyberg's conjecture of an emotional crisis between 1857 and 1860 and of some sort of homosexual "love affair" to explain it, and uses this assumption as a basis for the interpretation of some of the poems from which it was first conjectured. For the resulting hypothesis, sometimes for convenience stated as if it were fact, I ask only the minimum privilege of any such construction, a willing suspension of disbelief for long enough to make the statement possible. For convenience also, I write often as if the actual Whitman and the speaker in his poems were one and the same. Though I hope I may be permitted such shorthand devices in this brief paper, a full statement of these matters should of course constantly remind us that we are charting the drift of a highly active imagination, not reconstructing actual events.

[2] A version of this paper was read at the English Institute on September 6, 1960, as the first in a symposium on "Out of the Cradle."

[3] Floyd Stovall, "Main Drifts in Whitman's Poetry," *American Literature*, IV (1932), 3–21.

[4] *L'évolution*, pp. 344–359.

[5] Allen, p. 59. Cf. Gay Wilson Allen, *Walt Whitman Handbook* (Chicago, 1946), p. 124.

thought of death was clearly the chief threat his vision had to over-come. It did so not by doctrine nor any merely conceptual means but by lifting him to a Life that in its own nature contradicted death. He was relieved of his fear of death by becoming one with a life-force to which death simply *was not*. /11/

The logic of his position is stated by Emerson, whose service to the reader of Whitman is often to give conceptual definition to attitudes and insights which are too close to Whitman for definition, which he does not state because he lives them. Immortality, for Emerson, has nothing to do with duration or continuance. Rather it is "an intellectual quality," or even "an energy."

> He has it, and he alone, who gives life to all names, persons, things, where he comes. No religion, not the wildest mythology dies for him; no art is lost. He vivifies what he touches. Future state is an illusion for the ever-present state. It is not length of life, but depth of life. It is not duration, but a taking of the soul out of time, as all high action of the mind does: when we are living in the sentiments we ask no questions about time. The spiritual world takes place;—that which is always the same.[6]

Is this not equally the position of Whitman, whom Emerson might as well have been describing in this passage? In those first years Whitman could merge with an energy to which death was an irrelevance.

Of course we must translate a bit. Emerson's concept of a qualitative immortality is essentially ethical, a neo-stoicism, while Whitman's experience of it is an instinctive release of soul that carries no particular ethical condition except that one be capable of achieving it. One consequence is that the Life Whitman enters encompasses all time but is not out of time altogether, as is Emerson's. Lifted on its flood Whitman acquires a cosmic memory and a godlike prevision and can move backward and forward at will through the remotest ages. Unlike Emerson's Over-Soul, for which history is biography, the biography of Whitman's "Me myself" is history, but it is equally deathless since it is the life-force itself. Essentially, it brings him the same assurance, an ever-present Life beside which death is simply unreal.

Yet the force of this kind of transcendental vision derives partly from the fact that it *is* vision; Whitman holds to it so strongly because he is also aware that in his actual existence he continues to hover over the universal plunge into annihilation. Man's vision can

---

[6] "Immortality," *Letters and Social Aims*, in *Complete Works*, Centenary Edition (Boston and New York, 1904), VIII, 347.

transcend his mortal condition but cannot change it. Emerson confronted this fact and confessed he had nothing very helpful to say about it. "The event of death is always astounding; our philosophy never /12/ reaches, never possesses it; we are always at the beginning of our catechism; always the definition is yet to be made."[7] The best he could do was to repeat his ethical talisman, "Think on living." "Simply I have nothing to do" with "that question of another life." Whitman, I would say, takes the same position but because of the existential mode in which he writes can defend it more powerfully, if also more confusingly.

In Emerson's terms, it is the Reason that sees the ever-present immortality while the Understanding can see only the event of death. Both are right, but the poet by a fable can entice the Understanding out of its fears and so, as Plato put it, charm the child in the soul. This is the true function of those suggestions of a future state that certainly are to be found everywhere in these poems. Does Whitman, for example, believe in metempsychosis, as is so often asserted? It is hard to deny it, yet I would suggest that such a statement of the matter misses the point. These hints and guesses are bits of fable, *mythos*, "as-if" fragments scattered on the waters for the Understanding to cling to and support its unbelief. They are preparatory, instrumental, "indirect," intended not to assert anything directly but to throw the mind into the proper attitude to move beyond their metaphoric suggestions into the inwardness of pure truth. When Whitman exclaims of the dead, for example, "They are alive and well somewhere," his intention is not to tell us some fact but to stir us to feel about the dead *as if* that were the fact. All these hints of belief in the future that are thrown off from the first-phase poems, like sparkles from a pinwheel, are best taken as a measure of Whitman's confidence, exuberant enactments of the power and endless life which is his *now*. Essentially the faith from which they spring is self-sustaining and needs no doctrine to prop it; as Emerson said, the faith is the evidence. Life is; death is not: that is all Whitman knows or needs to know.

Such faith by inspection has the advantage that it is not tied to any formula and is not refutable by any argument. Its disadvantage is that it tends to die with the inspiration that brings it. The visionary gleam comes and goes by laws of its own, and each time it goes it leaves its votary face to face with the same spiritual emergency. It is not simply that the vision dies and is replaced by the unaltered facts it had denied. Vision itself is treacherous. A man may "loafe and invite" his

---

[7] *Journals* (Cambridge, Mass., 1910), IV, 343.

soul /13/ but he cannot predict or control what will accept the invitation. Vision may be demonic as well as transcendental, a nightmare confirmation of dread instead of a release of power and hope.

Both modes of vision are strong in Whitman from the beginning of his work; the stronger the poem, the more its dynamics are controlled by the battle between the two. In the 1855 poems the transcendental mode is dominant and the demonic recessive, but its concealed strength is great. It shows its teeth everywhere in "Song of Myself," something like one-fifteenth of the whole being of this character. More significant than its amount is its position. It touches with its threat the key passage on the meaning of the grass; it creeps in intermittently to darken the catalogues; and in the central sections it seizes control of the poem altogether and hammers at the poet with image after image of agony and defeat ("O Christ! My fit is mastering me!") until, cuffed and stunned, he wins a moment's respite and in that interval the transcendental vision sweeps back "replenished with supreme power." Even at the end, though no longer with power to alarm, a breath of nightmare returns and the poet must reconfirm his victory:

Of the turbid pool that lies in the autumn forest,
Of the moon that descends the steeps of the soughing twilight,
Toss, sparkles of day and dusk. . . . toss on the black stems that decay in
   the muck,
Toss to the moaning gibberish of the dry limbs.

I ascend from the moon . . . I ascend from the night,
And perceive of the ghastly glitter the sunbeams reflected,
And debouch to the steady and central from the offspring great or small.[8]

This dark element in the poem is by no means incidental; it is the enemy the hero exists to fight. "Song of Myself" is the epic of his victory. As with all Titanic heroes, as with the angels in *Paradise Lost*, his struggle is a bit unconvincing since we cannot really believe in the possibility of his defeat. But this appearance of invincibility is the

---

[8] All quotations in this paper are from the earliest published version of the poem cited: the 1855 version of "Song of Myself" and "The Sleepers," the 1860 version of "As I Ebb'd," that or the MS version of "Scented Herbage," and for "Out of the Cradle," the poem entitled "A Child's Reminiscence" which was published in the *Saturday Press* for December 27, 1859, and republished by Thomas O. Mabbott and Rollo G. Silver, University of Washington Quartos, No. 1 (Seattle, 1930). For clarity, however, I use the final titles. I have tried to read these poems without preconceptions imported from the more familiar revised versions, and I must ask anyone who would examine my conclusions to do the same.

true illusion, not the threat to it. That is supported not merely by the world trippers and askers around him but by the voices of doubt within him, "saying | That this was all folly." The hero's victory is /14/ earned; his power is needed; his air of omnipotence is the euphoria of a danger overcome.

If "Song of Myself" did not in itself tell us this, as it does, another poem of the 1855 edition makes it plain, the great companion piece to "Song of Myself" which Whitman eventually called "The Sleepers." That this poem also, like the other poems of this volume, brings us to the security which they were all written to celebrate should not prevent us from seeing that it does so by a very different road. The first line, "I wander all night with my vision," sounds like the start of a section of "Song of Myself," but we quickly see that this is not the same "I" nor the same vision: "Wandering and confused . . . . lost to myself . . . . ill-assorted . . . . contradictory." This "I" is not "Myself" but is "lost to myself." It is a night consciousness, troubled, confused, disembodied, will-less and disorganized like the mind in sleep. The expansive energy of "Song of Myself" is withdrawn from this poem; the speaker here is passive and powerless. He is therefore *exposed* in a way the hero of "Song of Myself" was not. He encounters at once images of death and defeat—

> The wretched features of ennuyees, the white features of corpses, the livid
> faces of drunkards, the sick-gray faces of onanists,
> The gashed bodies on battlefields, the insane in their strong-doored
> rooms, the sacred idiots . . . .

Eighteen of the twenty-five classes of sleeper specified in the first twenty-six lines of the poem are disturbing in some way, samples of evil, distress, or death. The center of this poem, we soon see, is not life but death. The chief sleeper is the transcendental assurance of life that controls "Song of Myself." That poem had said, not without a struggle, "The dead are not dead." "The Sleepers" says, "Here they lie." Quite deliberately, I think, Whitman here permits to speak the darker under-consciousness which his waking vision had put down but which remained and must remain part of his truth.

The chief evidence for this conclusion is the long section of the /15/ poem, following the introductory description of the sleepers as they lie "stretched and still," in which the poet somnambulistically enters and becomes a succession of dreams. Though the fiction of this section is that these are a miscellaneous sample of the dreams of a num-

ber of people, we cannot get very far into it without realizing that
they look more like the dreams of one consciousness. Certain points
can be made about them: (1) They are connected by numerous ties of
detail, action, and mood and can be made with little forcing to tell a
continuous story, a story which, as is appropriate to the unconscious
autobiography that emerges in such dreams, is essentially an oedipal
one. (2) Their dominant mood is one of anxiety and guilt; one after
another they present images of disaster and loss. Even when the poet
makes a visible effort to extricate himself from their oppression it
continues to control him, modulating at last into the murderous an-
ger that is concomitant with such feelings. (3) Certain of the individual dreams seem to offer a deliberate contrast to "Song of Myself."
During the sermon that concludes "Song of Myself," for example, the
prophet-god says to his disciple,

> Long have you timidly waded, holding a plank by the shore,
> Now I will you to be a bold swimmer,
> To jump off in the midst of the sea, and rise again and nod to me and
>   shout, and laughingly dash with your hair.

Now this bold swimmer returns, only to be dashed on the rocks and
killed, while the dreamer watches helplessly from the shore. And a
few lines earlier, when the dreamer has become a shroud to wrap a
body in the grave, the grave does not "multiply what has been con-
fided" to it, nor does the corpse rise.

> It seems to me that everything in the light and air ought to be happy;
> Whoever is not in his coffin and the grave, let him know he has
>   enough.

In this part of the poem Whitman does not merely return to the
thought of death but reveals through these dreams some of the reasons for his preoccupation with it. He taps a part of the something-
settled matter in his heart whose threat permanently underlay his
transcendental vision. The great upsurge of creative activity, Catel
points out, which produced the 1855 *Leaves of Grass* partially re-
solved the conflicts that led to it, but only partially, "for the work of
art, even if a substitute for action, does not exhaust the forces that lie
/16/ in a dream-filled sleep within us" (p. 8). In "The Sleepers" these
forces stir.

I must not leave this poem, however, without noting the chief
fact about it, namely that these dreams *are* dreams. Their content,

which I am suggesting is as real as anything in Whitman, can reach such full expression only because it does so in the guise of dreams, just as the theme of death can enter this poem with so little resistance because these dead are not dead, but sleepers merely. I have been stressing one element of the consciousness that controls this poem because it comes closest to the dark or demonic underside of Whitman's vision which I am concerned to bring out, but there is another element, strong from the beginning, which takes over after the dream sequence is over and erases its anxieties in an all-embracing consolation. This might be called the maternal element, the thought of sleep not as death or self-loss but as rest and restoration. Here certainly one cannot maintain that Whitman does not assert a belief in the future, for the poem rests for its consolation entirely on the analogy of death and night. As sleep banishes the cares that infest the day, so the dead "pass the invigoration of the night and the chemistry of the night and awake" to new life. I will not try to worry Whitman's beautiful fable into consistency with my general position, though I think it could be done, but simply note that this night-myth of restoration, like the day-myth of an unwounded wholeness that needs no restoration, is a total one. Both combine with all of the 1855 poems to celebrate life's perfection.

II

The poems of 1856 and the poems in the Valentine MSS. which Bowers[9] dates 1857 do not evidence any basic change of position. Whitman continues to affirm life and immortality, proclaims the perfection of nature, including the body and all its functions, announces his perfect happiness, and begins a systematic program of applying his affirmative insight to every aspect of the world around him. A few poems of 1857, however, strike a darker note. "I Sit and Look Out" is among this number, as are "A Hand-Mirror," "Confession and Warning," "Of Him I Love Day and Night," and one or two more. Thoughts of guilt, evil, and death emerge in these short lyrics with- /17/ out any compensating affirmation except the context of other poems. We notice also that a largely 1857 poem of affirmation like "A Song of Joys" is in places more wildly exuberant, more desperately aggressive in tone than anything that had preceded it. These and other small indications suggest that the wave of confidence that crested in 1855 is beginning to falter and break of its own momentum. The blow that

---

[9] Fredson Bowers, *Whitman's Manuscripts:* Leaves of Grass *(1860)* (Chicago, 1955).

apparently struck the man in 1858 or 1859 precipitated a crisis in his poems and no doubt deepened it, but some crisis or other was bound to occur in any case.

For some reason, perhaps simply that Whitman was busy, no poems can be certainly dated 1858. 1859 was the Calamus year. Of the twenty-six poems in the Valentine MSS. that were probably written in 1859, twenty-two are Calamus poems, whereas almost none that can be dated earlier are clearly of this kind. The "Calamus fragrance," to use Bowers' expression, that sifts into the two program poems of the 1860 edition, "Starting From Paumanok" and "So Long," was apparently added in 1859. Add the half a dozen or so more Calamus poems that appeared in the 1860 edition, all of which may well date from 1859 also, and you have just about all the Calamus material in *Leaves of Grass*. In 1859, give or take a few months, Whitman wrote nearly all the Calamus poems he was to write and wrote little else. In view of these facts, his later contention that these poems were part of a considered program toward which he was moving from the beginning seems highly unlikely. Rather, something utterly unforeseen has irrupted into his work, sweeping the rest of it aside and engrossing both man and poet. What the source of this new thing was can be conjectured, though we do not know the biographical facts. Whitman had some sort of unhappy love relation with a man,[10] one that brought him a brief glimpse of happiness and then plunged him into bitter suffering. His suffering, we may believe, was intensified by the confirmation of his darkest suspicions about his own nature. To someone who, like his time and place, was in many ways as unsophisticated and even puritanical in sexual matters /18/ as Whitman seems to have been, for all his big talk, this decisive demonstration of his own difference came as a bewildering shock.[11]

The consequences for his poetry of this crisis are spelled out for us in one of the three "summation" poems that came out of this year,

---

[10] "In spite of a few moments of happiness that Whitman may possibly have had in a love affair [in 1858 or 1859], it is highly probable that after all *he was not talking of any erotic relationship,* that it never actually developed that far; moreover *I suspect that, after all, Whitman never actually had any such experience during his whole life, in spite of his homosexual bent*" (Schyberg-Allen, p. 167, Schyberg's italics). See the whole passage.

[11] I am glad to acknowledge a debt here to an acute article by Clark Griffith, "Sex and Death: The Significance of Whitman's *Calamus* Themes," *Philological Quarterly*, XXXIX (1960), 18–38. While I agree with Mr. Griffith on the occasion and the depth of Whitman's Calamus crisis, his explanation of its severity seems to me too narrowly intellectual. It was not the mere refutation of his sex program that devastated Whitman; it was the toppling of his entire structure of transcendental assurance.

"As I Ebb'd With the Ocean of Life,"[12] which reads like a conscious repudiation of "Song of Myself." The central figure is the poet—and in early notebook drafts, as well as in the Preface, the hero of the 1855 edition was the poet—engaged in the same search for "types" from which he had once gathered such a rich harvest. Nature ironically offers him the trash on the water's edge, and with a shock of recognition he finds in it the emblem of his present state, namely his inability any more to see saving emblems. The poem is a farewell to his poetic vocation—premature, as it turned out, but nonetheless deeply sincere at the time. Instead of a "liberating god" and his triumphant songs of celebration, he and his "arrogant poems" are nothing, "debris." The "real Me" he thought he had courted and won in "Song of Myself" "still stands untouched, untold, altogether unreached." Instead, he is "held by the eternal self of me that threatens to get the better of me, and stifle me." He and the "Me myself" are opposed, not in union; in Melville's words, his identity has come back in horror. Now he sees the utter folly of his claim to be the master and interpreter of nature: "I perceive I have not really understood any thing—not a single object—and that no man ever can." He is and always has been in the hands of mysterious great forces that save him as they please and drop him as they please.

The poem bears every mark of having been written by a man in deep grief, as indeed it was. Strangely, the whole scene is in distress and mourns with the poet even while it denies him. The wound of separation pains both alike. Its cause is mysterious, but we vaguely /19/ sense some unspecified hurt behind the vastation they lament. All we know is that the blow has been struck and he finds himself here, crushed and abandoned. The poem denies the claims of "Song of Myself" much more radically than did "The Sleepers." Whitman confronts annihilation once more, not in the guise of dreams but in waking earnest, just as if his visions of life had never been. "(See! from my dead lips the ooze exuding at last!)" The transcendental cycle is over. He hopes, it is true, that "the flow will return" and that he "will yet sing, someday," but this must be read as prayer, not conviction. Though he may yet in a measure recover his spirits and his singing strength, the sweeping affirmative power from which his first-phase poems had proceeded will never return in that form again.

---

12 The other two being "Scented Herbage of My Breast" and "Out of the Cradle." The order in which I discuss these poems is the one that best fits my argument. Actually, "As I Ebb'd" was quite possibly written last, at a time when, as in "Out of the Cradle," Whitman had reached enough perspective on his crisis to permit him to treat it in poetry. The ebb and flow of the emotional life does not follow the tidy patterns that are necessary for its exposition.

Rather he finds a way out on the other side of his despair itself. We can watch this happen in one of the most extraordinary poems he ever wrote, "Scented Herbage of My Breast." This, like "As I Ebb'd," is another farewell to his vocation as the poet of Life—indeed, to life itself. The poet, anticipating the death he now welcomes, thinks of his "leaves," no longer as the grass growing even on graves to show "there is really no death," but as delicate "tomb-leaves" that will survive for a while the killing winter, as he cannot, to bloom perennially from his grave and tell "a few" of the suffering from which they sprang. The poem is itself a "breast leaf" of the kind it describes, a solitary cry of grief like the song of the bird in "Out of the Cradle." It soon drops its elegiac tone and speaks out directly.

> O aching and throbbing! O these hungering desires!
> Surely one day they will be pacified—all will be accomplished
> O I know not what you mean—you are not happiness— you are often
>   too bitter![13]

The interpolated assurance here, an echo of his old faith, is now purely a desperate expression of need. The true ground of his pain is the recognition that *nothing* will pacify his desires, that love is necessarily something unaccomplished. Why this must be so becomes clear when we remember what Whitman meant by love. He has been shown at last what real love is only to find that it is something that cannot and must not hope for fulfillment. Since love is also the only real thing in life, the heart of this poem is a genuinely tragic recognition: to live is to love and to love is to lose. Love is the beginning /20/ of life and also its end. Whitman has moved in this poem beyond the personal torment of such a Calamus poem as "Hours Continuing Long" to a universal insight.

Not that "Scented Herbage" is any the less passionate for that; it is the most passionate love poem he ever wrote. His recognition lifts him to a kind of exaltation. Death becomes beautiful to him, not because it promises him the fulfillment life denies him, but simply because his love is so strong that it must go somewhere and this is the only way open to it. Since to love is to lose, "the high Soul of lovers welcomes death most." Life reserves for the lover its final secret, that the "real reality" is love and death. The poem rises to meet the new knowledge that the needs of the heart are not met by life, that man is born for defeat. The only course open to him, then, is to consent to what must be, cast off his demand for life and fear of death and go to

---

[13] MS version, Bowers, p. 70.

meet his fate halfway. "Death or life I am then indifferent—my Soul declines to prefer." Its exaltation is the exaltation of passing beyond hope and illusion to a knowledge of what life and death finally are. "The readiness is all."

> He is King of Harm
> Who hath suffered Him.

I have suggested that at the peak of his transcendental vision Whitman knew immortality by direct insight, with no need for the aid of myth or doctrine. Something like that is true at this second peak also. The knowledge to which this poem rises of love and death as the real reality is without intermediary or metaphor.

> Emblematic and capricious blades, I leave you—now you serve me not,
> Away! I will say what I have to say, by itself. . . .

If there is such a thing as tragic Reason, then this is its poem. Death is welcomed, not because of any promise or myth, nor through mere despair of life, but simply in and for itself, because it is real.

It would be pleasant to ring down the curtain on this high note, as on one of the soaring fifth-act arias which this poem much resembles, but with thirty years of Whitman's work and at least one of his greatest poems still to come that would hardly be accurate. This kind of vision, too, like all vision, has its laws and limits. One difference between art and life is that the tragic hero can remain frozen on his peak of exaltation while the actual man must come down from such /21/ heights and go on living. Whitman, I would guess, found it much harder to hold to his tragic vision in its purity than he had found it to maintain his transcendental one. It seems likely that only an extraordinary stress of feeling brought him to the point of such vision at all; as that stress diminished he never quite reached it again, though if my thesis is correct its impact decisively controls all his later work.

A "dialectical" pattern of emotional development much like that which reached its definitive artistic expression in "When Lilacs Last," I am arguing, was a central pattern in his own experience, *lived through* by him well before he ever looked into Hegel. From the simultaneous knowledge of the ever-present immortality and of the event of death, the transcendental assurance and its demonic shadow, each dominant in turn according to the strength or weakness of his vision of safety, he moved, under the impact of his awakening to love and death, to a new knowledge both sadder and surer. If there was loss in the collapse of his total triumph over death, there was gain in the certainty that no further shock of awakening could come to him; now he *knew.* The ground of the recovery which, as Asselineau argues, the very publication of the 1860 edition attests[14] was thus laid by the same discovery that destroyed the overconfidence out of which his poems had begun. The knowledge it brought him, the stoic privilege it gave him of being one of those that know the truth, became the rock on which his mature equilibrium thereafter was founded. His wound-dressing years tested and confirmed it but did not create it.

A similar process of confirmation can be traced in the poems. Since it brought him at last to assurances of immortality that superficially resemble his first-phase proclamations and which in his final philosophic phase, when he wished to insist on the synthetic unity of his whole work, he was glad to merge with them, it is important to insist that they do not have the same basis. Whitman did not just "recover his serenity," if by that we mean that all became as it had been. The greatest disservice the later Whitman did himself was to lead us to overlook and belittle the significance of his deepest crisis. After he "had been to touch the great death," he could no longer reach, and no longer needed, the power to affirm that death did not exist. He never again looked for final satisfaction to life, nor did he again fall /22/ under the old terror of annihilation.

What happened instead was that he began instinctively to build on his new insight, as he had his old, with imaginative materials, to bolster and confirm it, if also somewhat to ease it, with "carols of death" more suitable to the needs of the Understanding. Since metaphors for the Understanding are the lifeblood of poetry it appears foolish to complain of this process and indeed I do not. Many of its results, such as "Darest Thou Now, O Soul" or "Whispers of Heavenly Death" or "Reconciliation," not to mention "When Lilacs Last," are particularly beautiful, so that one would be grateful for Whitman's Calamus crisis if it had led to nothing else. It is a measure of his achievement in "Scented Herbage" to suggest that such poems are in any sense deficient by comparison. On a level just below them is a poem like "Passage to India," one of the best of Whitman's second-best poems, where the metaphor has begun to shrink and harden into a relatively conventional doctrine of the soul's immortal safety on "the seas of God" beyond the grave. We can catch this mythologizing process at its inception and perhaps at its best in "Out of the Cradle."

---

[14] *L'évolution,* p. 113; *The Evolution,* p. 114.

III

In "Out of the Cradle" Whitman has contrived to tell his whole story and even to go beyond it. The long one-sentence "pre-verse" is intended to establish the basic fiction of the poem. The poet will tell us of something long past, he suggests, which now for some reason comes over his memory. By this distancing device he contrives to win some artistic and personal control over his material. In most versions the distinction of the poet that is and the boy that was is made sharp and distinct:

> I, chanter of pains and joys, uniter of here and hereafter . . .
> A reminiscence sing.

Such a bardic line implies firm poetic control, emotion recollected in tranquillity. But neither this line nor the following one is in the 1859 version, where the poet therefore seems much more under the spell of the memories that have seized him:

> A man—yet by these tears a little boy again,
> Throwing myself on the sand, I,
> Confronting the waves, sing.

/23/ What has actually seized him, of course, is the meaning *now* to him of these images, so much so that in the first version he has a hard time keeping the presentness of his feelings from bursting through and destroying his narrative fiction.

Nevertheless, the reminiscent mode of the poem greatly enlarges its range by permitting him to bring his whole life to bear on it. As a poem of loss and awakening it goes back even to his very earliest loss and awakening, the "primal" separation of the child from the mother. Though this theme is stressed at once by the poet, especially in the original version, one must avoid reductiveness here. This layer of the poem underlies the whole and already predicts its shape, but it is not the completed structure. From it comes, however, a powerful metaphor for the awakening that is the main subject.

The boy, leaving his bed, finds himself wandering in a strange dark world like something out of Blake, a haunted borderland between shore and sea, here and hereafter, conscious and unconscious. In its troubled restlessness it resembles the moonlit swamp that is glimpsed for a moment in "Song of Myself," or some of the dreamscenes in "The Sleepers." We sense here, especially in the 1859 version, which is more dark and troubled throughout than the final one,

the same dumb, unassuageable grief as in "As I Ebb'd." It also is a
wounded world, impotently twining and twisting with the pain of
some obscure fatality. Here there is even less visible occasion for such
agony, since the chief actor is not a broken poet but a curious child.
The poem is heavy with the man's foreknowledge of what the child,
now born, must go through. Like the star in "When Lilacs Last,"
however, the scene also has something to tell, some "drowned secret" which it is struggling to utter. It does not merely mourn a loss,
like the seascape in "As I Ebb'd," but also hints of something to be
found.

What has drawn the boy from his infantile security into this par-
turient midnight is a bird. In a flashback the poet tells of the brief
May idyll of Two Together, the sudden loss of the she-bird, and the
wonderful song of woe that followed, drawing the boy back night
after night to listen until the night came when he awakened to its
meaning. Then it seemed to him that the bird was a messenger, an
interpreter, singing on behalf of the new world he had entered to tell
him its secret. This secret is really two secrets, that the meaning of
life is love and that he is to be its poet. The song releases the love and
/24/ the songs of love in his own heart, which he now realizes has
long been ready and waiting for this moment; he awakes and
ecstatically dedicates himself to this service.

Yet, bewilderingly, this discovery of what life means and what he
is for at once plunges him into new trouble and doubt; he finds himself once more groping for something unknown, and is not released
until the voice of the sea whispers him a very different secret, the
word death. This *double* awakening provides criticism with its chief
problem in this poem. It is true that the boy's spiritual development
is dramatically consistent and requires no explanation from outside
the poem, but it is complex and rapid, an extreme example of dramatic foreshortening. Since it is also intensely personal, the biographical framework I have sketched helps to make its meaning clear.

To put the matter summarily, in the boy's awakening Whitman
has fused all his own awakenings together, with the result that his
poem moves in one night over a distance which he had taken forty
years of life to cover. The emotional foreground, of course, is occu-
pied by the tragic awakening of 1859, the discovery of love not merely
as a passion for one particular being rather than an appetite for everything in general, but also as inherently unsatisfied. Love and grief are
one. The bird's story is Whitman's story, distanced and disguised,
but it is also man's. The outsetting bard of love will be the bard of
unsatisfied love because there is no other kind.

But here we encounter a difficulty, for in many of the other poems of 1859 Whitman had suggested that his awakening to love had stopped his poems and ended his poetic career. Of course he could hardly have overlooked the fact that his crisis did arouse him to new poems and to some of his best. Certainly he was proud of this poem, immediately printed it and followed it with one of his self-written reviews announcing that he would not be mute any more. Perhaps we may read a special meaning into his selection of this poem as the first public evidence of his return to song. In this "reminiscence" of the birth of his poetic vocation he is actually celebrating its recovery. The process of relieving his pain in song has now proceeded so far, past "death's outlet" songs like "Hours Continuing Long" and "As I Ebb'd," past a poem of first recognition like "Scented Herbage," that he can now begin to see that the deathblow to his old "arrogant poems" is proving to be a lifeblow to new and better if more sorrowful ones, and so for the first time, in the guise of a reminiscence, he /25/ can make not just his grief, but its transmutation into the relief of song the subject of his singing.

In the measure that he recovers his poetic future he also recovers his past. His sense of returning powers naturally picks up and blends with his memories of that other awakening, whenever and whatever it was, that led to the poems of 1855. In the boy's joy he draws on and echoes his first awakening, the ecstatic union of self and soul celebrated in "Song of Myself," when he *had* felt a thousand songs starting to life within him in response to the "song of Two Together." Overlaid on that is his second dark awakening to the truth of "two together no more" which had at first appeared to end his singing. If we thus provisionally disentangle the strands that Whitman has woven together we can understand better why the song of the bird must plunge the boy almost simultaneously into ecstasy and despair.

The steps of this process are obscured for us in the final version by Whitman's deletion of a crucial stanza that explains why the boy needs a word from the sea when he already has so much from the bird. After the lines

> O give me some clue!
> O if I am to have so much, let me have more!

the original version continued as follows:

> O a word! O what is my destination?
> O I fear it is henceforth chaos!

O how joys, dreads, convolutions, human shapes, and all shapes, spring
    as from graves around me!
O phantoms! You cover all the land and all the sea!
O I cannot see in the dimness whether you smile or frown upon me!
O vapor, a look, a word! O well-beloved!
O you dear women's and men's phantoms!

This stanza or something similar appears in all editions of "Out of the
Cradle" until the last version of 1881, when Whitman was twenty
years away from his poem. Perhaps he dropped it then because he
felt it spoke too plainly from the emotions of 1859 and was not in
keeping with what his poem had become. That it was not necessary
to the success of the poem is proved by the success the poem has had
without it, yet its omission greatly changes the total effect. The quality of the boy's need is lightened to a more usual adolescent distress
and the sea's answer becomes the kind of grave reassurance charac-
/26/ teristic of the later Whitman. In the original version the boy is
not just distressed, he is desperate with the desperation of the man of
1859. The first act of his awakened poet's vision has been to abort and
produce a frightening chaos. Instead of the triumphant vision of Life
which Whitman himself had known, when the whole world smiled
on its conquering lover, nothing rises now before the outsetting bard
but a dim phantasmagoria of death-shapes. It is almost impossible not
to read this passage as coming from the poet himself rather than from
the boy—indeed, Whitman was right to cut it, it *is* out of keeping—
for these "dear women's and men's phantoms" are surely dear because they are those of the men and women and the whole world
that had *already* started to life for him in his poems, their life the ed-
dying of his living soul, but are now strengthless ghosts, like the
power of vision from which their life had come. This is the "terrible
doubt of appearances" that had plagued him from the beginning,
now revived and confirmed by his new crisis. Whitman here openly
transfers to the boy the man's despair.

With this background it should not be hard to see that the answer
the sea gives to the despair characteristic of 1859 is the answer characteristic of 1859. Its essential quality is the same tragic acceptance as in
"Scented Herbage," a knowledge of death not as consolation or
promise, still less as mere appearance, but as reality, the "real reality"
that completes the reality of love in the only way in which it can be
completed. In the language of Thoreau, the sea is a "realometer" that
says, "this is, and no mistake." The lift her answer brings is like that
of "Scented Herbage," the lift of naming the whole truth and so

passing beyond illusion to a consent to fate. A sign that this is so is the
sea's taciturnity. The thrush's beautiful song of death in 1865, weav-
ing a veil of life-illusion over the same hard truth and so easing it for
us, is not present here; simply the word, the thing itself. In this stark
directness, again, the kinship is to "Scented Herbage" rather than to
"When Lilacs Last."

Yet certainly the fact that this word also, like the bird's song of
love and the boy's despair, is ascribed to a dramatic character makes
a profound difference. The sea as dramatic character in this poem has
two phases. In the earlier part, before the boy turns to her for his answer, she is a background voice blending with the drama of bird and
boy but essentially not a part of it. She has an ancient sorrow of her
own which leaves her no grief to spare for this small incident on her
/27/ shores. She does not share the egocentric fallacy of boy and bird,
in which even moon, wind, and shadows join in futile sympathy. In
this part of the poem she is the same sea as in "As I Ebb'd," the
"fierce old mother" who "endlessly cries for her castaways"—all her
castaways, not just these—the deep ocean of life and death that rolls
through all things.

Of course, behind every detail of the poem, including this one, we
feel the poet's shaping power, creating a symbolical language for the
life of his own mind. In this kind of subjective drama the author is all
the characters; bird, boy, and sea are one and join in a grief that is at
bottom the same because it is his own. But Whitman has now seen
through the Emersonian illusion that the power of the poet prophe-
sies a victory for the man. Where "Song of Myself" had dramatized
the omnipotence of bardic vision, "Out of the Cradle" dramatizes
the discovery that the power of the bard is only to sing his own limits.
Like the bird in Marianne Moore's poem, his singing is mighty because he is caged. As a dramatic character, then, the sea is the Not-
Me, Fate, Karma, that-which-cannot-be-changed. As such she dominates the scene, which is all, as Kenneth Burke would say, under her
aegis, but she does not share in its temporal passions.

At the end, however, she condescends to reveal herself and changes
from the ground of the question to the answer. The change is not so
much in the sea as in the boy. As before, he hears when he is ready to
listen; the sea has been speaking all the time. Even the bird, in the
early version, heard her and responded with continued song. Before
he can hear her the boy must finish his egocentric cycle and pass from
his hybristic promise to sing "clearer, louder, and more sorrowful"
songs than the bird's to his despairing recognition that there is no
good in him. The sign that he is ready is the question itself. Then the

sea approaches and whispers as privately for him, revealing the secret which will release him from passion to perception. What she shows him is, I have suggested, no consoling revelation but simply reality. Yet the fact that this answer is now felt to come from the sea, from the heart of the Not-Me that has defeated Whitman's arrogant demands for another Me, suggests that the division between him and his world is not final after all, that the separation both have suffered can still be healed. The elemental forces of "As I Ebb'd" have fused with the perception of reality in "Scented Herbage" to form a new Thou, in Buber's language—no longer the tousled mistress Whitman had /28/ ordered around in "Song of Myself," certainly, but a goddess who will speak to him when he is ready to accept her on her own terms. Then he can hear in the voice of the sea the voice of a mother, a figure as we know "always near and always divine" to him. The real reality of "Scented Herbage" has acquired a local habitation and a name, has gathered around itself life and numenosity, and Whitman is well on his way by this dark path to replace the Comrade who had deserted him on the open road.

Richard Chase

"Out of the Cradle" as a Romance*

I am not entirely happy with the word "romance" as applied to "Out of the Cradle Endlessly Rocking," but it is the best word I can think of for my purpose. I am sure its meaning will not be immediately clear. After all, "Out of the Cradle" is not a poem about sexual love and courtship; it is not a medieval allegory; it has no knights in shining armor and no chivalry to speak of. I use the word "romance" as I did in my book on the American novel,† to suggest certain literary qualities which are characteristically, though not exclusively, American, and to suggest, therefore, that Whitman's poem has certain things in common with the writings of Poe, Hawthorne, Melville, and others among our fictionists, beyond what has been noticed by such careful comparative critics as F. O. Matthiessen.

In keeping with my definition of American "romance" in my book on the novel, I use the term to suggest that "Out of the Cradle" is one of the many American works of literature whose chief moods are those of idyl and melodrama. I intend to suggest that the poem achieves its own finished form only by means of /53/ disrupting into irreconcilable and extreme contradictions the universe of which it speaks. And I intend to suggest that although the main question raised in the poem is nothing less complex and interesting than the origin of the poet's genius, the answer the poet gives us is too pat and strikes us as only a half truth, if a truth at all. Finally, I intend to suggest that the world of moral experience set forth in "Out of the Cradle" is a treacherous world to live in. I had better hasten to add, though it

* Reprinted from *The Presence of Walt Whitman: Selected Papers from the English Institute* (New York: Columbia University Press, 1962), pp. 52–71, by permission.
† *The American Novel and Its Tradition* (New York, 1957).

may sound like a paradox, that I think "Out of the Cradle" a great poem, and one of Whitman's best. There is no reason why a master of his language should not transmute into poetic form some very dubious materials, and Whitman has done this in "Out of the Cradle." Even so, the poem falls short of the tragic utterance it tries to be and remains somewhere in the second rank behind the world's greatest poems. In doing so it aligns itself with many of the best American poems and novels.

But before pursuing these matters further, let me set down some notes toward a general view of Whitman. In *Democratic Vistas* Whitman speaks of the need for a moral and spiritual regeneration in America. He allots to the poet, or as he is oddly called, the literatus, a highly important place. We are told the main characteristics of the literatus and of the national literature he will produce. The literatuses of the future, not too surprisingly, will resemble Walt Whitman, or rather—and this is an important distinction—they will resemble Whitman as he thought of himself in his public role as a prophet and teacher. The image of the literatus *Democratic Vistas* projects is of a poet who furnishes archetypes (Whitman's word) for an optimistic, "orbic," "kosmical" America, an America devoted to "a strong-fibred joyous- /54/ ness and faith, and the sense of health *al fresco*." There is little enough here to remind us of the Whitman we have come in recent years to understand—the real Whitman, the divided, covert, musing, "double," furtive man, poet and showman, who wrote the poems we prize. These poems of course are by no means always orbic or kosmical. For neither Whitman himself nor his disciples ever quite succeeded in making him into the prophet or the teacher-philosopher. This is most fortunate, for otherwise we would have lost the Whitman who with his bewitching combination of ego and doubt, of charlatanism and sincerity, of comic self-regard and wistful nostalgia, of neurosis and health wrote poems such as "Song of Myself," "Crossing Brooklyn Ferry," and "As I Ebb'd with the Ocean of Life." "Our Walt Whitman," says Leslie Fiedler, "is the slyest of artificers . . . he is a player with illusion; his center is a pun on the self; his poetry is a continual shimmering on the surfaces of concealment and revelation that is at once pathetic and comical." Mr. Fiedler goes on to say that Whitman was not, or not in essence, the tribal bard. "He was only a man, ridden by impotence and anxiety, by desire and guilt, furtive and stubborn and half-educated. That he became the world's looked-for, ridiculous darling is astonishing enough; that he remained a poet through it all is scarcely credible." These words are from Mr. Fiedler's excellent essay called "Images of Walt Whitman."

For a further description of the poet who is here being called *"our Walt Whitman,"* one might look into the pages of the first book really to understand this poet, Constance Rourke's *American Humor*. But there is also Randall Jarrell's essay entitled "Some Lines from Whitman" (in his *Poetry and the Age*) /55/ and my own book of 1955, *Walt Whitman Reconsidered*. If these writings delineate "our Walt Whitman," why then is my book, or at least the chapter on "Song of Myself," described by Mr. Willard Thorp (in *Eight American Authors*, published by MLA) as "to say the least, aberrant"? I would have been grateful to Mr. Thorp if he had said "unorthodox" instead of "aberrant." For there has indeed been an orthodoxy among most Whitman scholars. It is not the orthodoxy of the original disciples and of Edgar Lee Masters, that makes Whitman a messiah and tribal bard. It is the orthodoxy of the history-of-ideas approach to literature that makes Whitman a philosopher or possibly even a theologian of the mystic variety (not that vain Walt wouldn't have been pleased by the compliment). This approach is to be found, for example, in James E. Miller's recent *A Critical Guide to Leaves of Grass*, which, in taking Whitman for a religious mystic, descends from such different works as Richard M. Bucke's *Cosmic Consciousness* and Hart Crane's *The Bridge*. I would think that the critical reader who embarks on a reading of Whitman, as Mr. Miller does, with a copy of Evelyn Underhill's *Mysticism: A Study in the Nature and Development of Man's Spiritual Consciousness* at hand, would do well to have also at hand a copy of Tocqueville's *Democracy in America* and of Miss Rourke's book mentioned above. I would think that instead of looking for the Immortal and the Ineffable, the Cosmic and the Mystical, he might look, as in his imperfect way Whitman looked, at the realities of a democratic civilization.

Or consider as another example of the purely intellectualist approach, Gay Wilson Allen's *Walt Whitman Handbook*. With all its talk of immanence and emanation, acosmism and cosmo- /56/ theism, pantheism and panpsychism, the book never gets around to a discussion of Whitman's real subject, which is the plight and destiny of the self. It is impossible to sympathize with Mr. Allen's contention that "an exhaustive comparative study needs to be made of the relations of Whitman's thought to the [Great] Chain of Being." Poor old Walt, he had never heard of the Great Chain of Being. His leading conceptions are the self, equality, and contradiction—appropriate preoccupations for the poet of American democracy. What use had he, in a democratic culture, for the philosophic counterpart of European hierarchies? Surely we shall not take too seriously, although generations of scholars have, Whitman's fancy references to Hegel, Plato, and other philosophers.

But to return to the projected literatus of *Democratic Vistas,* he resembles in one respect at least the deepest and most genuine Whitman. Only people unfamiliar with Whitman's own poems will be surprised when he remarks that "in the future of these States must arise poets immenser far, and make great poems of death." There are indeed many great poems of death in American literature, both in verse and prose, although none of the authors—Poe, Emily Dickinson, Melville, Stephen Crane, to mention a few—resembles the literatus any more than does Whitman himself—I mean Whitman the genuine, the immortal poet. Among these great poems of death belong "Out of the Cradle Endlessly Rocking."

Before we come to a closer examination of this poem, let us consider its place in the Whitman canon. I am aware that my idea of this is at odds with what is or for a long time was the conventional view of Whitman's development. This view (and /57/ I believe that in many academic halls it still is the conventional view) was well expressed in 1932 in an essay by Mr. Floyd Stovall called "Main Drifts in Whitman's Poetry." The Parringtonian title of Mr. Stovall's essay is not amiss, for he does not trace Whitman's development by looking at the poet and his poems in their sheer naked insistent quiddity. He traces it, as he himself says, by following the currents of Whitman's "thought." Since the older one is the more "thought" one has had a chance to acquire, it is a foregone conclusion that Whitman's writing, as it goes through its various stages, gets better and better. As Mr. Stovall sees it, we have three stages in Whitman's poetry. The first is characterized by "Song of Myself," with its brash but unthinking self-assertion and its unexamined optimism; in this first stage Whitman, though thirty-six when "Song of Myself" was published, is still "immature." The second stage is announced by "Out of the Cradle," a tragic love poem in which a sobered Whitman confronts death and gains a mature or whole view of life. "Death is the consoler," wrote Mr. Stovall, "the clue to man's destiny, because it is the divine complement of human imperfection through which love is made complete and immortal." (But where, one might ask, does the poem make love complete and immortal? It seems rather to say that love is unstable and without an object—unless indeed that object is death in and for itself, for death is not presented in this poem as the gateway to the immortal or as a compensatory term in the rhythm of life.) As I have said, "Out of the Cradle" does not strike me as a tragic poem, and people who call it that seem to use the word either in the ordinary but unsatisfactory sense, as referring to anything that is very sad, or in some vaguely honorific sense. /58/

During the second stage, the argument continues, Whitman's "thought" waxed and deepened as he became less interested in the self and more interested in the community and the fate of mankind. In the third stage, characterized best by "Passage to India," Whitman grew more spiritual and conservative and aware of the divine, universal plan of things. As Mr. Stovall says, "Love, already national in scope, now reached out to include the entire world." I do not myself see why love reaching out to include the entire world should necessarily be regarded as a good thing. Diffuseness, whether of love or anything else, was always Whitman's Waterloo as a poet. And far from being a step forward, Whitman's gradually slackening sense of the self and its dialectical relations with the not-self, a slackening which we begin to observe in his work after the 1855 edition, was the beginning of the end of his greatness as a poet. The great poems of Whitman's middle period—"Out of the Cradle," "As I Ebb'd," "When Lilacs Last in the Dooryard Bloom'd"—are not an "advance" over "Song of Myself"; they are merely *different*, in style and tone. It would be just as true (that is, not true at all) to call them a "retreat" from "Song of Myself." Apart from their value as poetry, they seem really, in their elegiac mood, to constitute a kind of swan song, for although Whitman wrote much fine verse in later life his period of best accomplishment was surely between "Song of Myself" and "When Lilacs Last."

That "Out of the Cradle" is one of Whitman's best poems we do not need to spend much more time in affirming. Any sympathetic reader, not too encased in the Eliot-Pound tradition, must surely feel the magnificence of this poem, and I think this may be felt and admitted even by readers who, like myself, do /59/ not care for more cosmic and universalized utterances like "Salut au Monde" and "Passage to India." In those poems reality is diffuse and homogenized. In "Out of the Cradle" reality may be elusive, but once we have got hold of it, it is seen to be particular and concrete, besides having universal significance. Perhaps these qualities are what led Swinburne to call the poem "faultless" and "noble" and what inspired Henry James (as Edith Wharton tells us in an oft-quoted passage) to read aloud one evening from "Song of Myself" and then, his voice filling "the hushed room like an organ adagio," proceed to "the mysterious music of 'Out of the Cradle,' reading, or rather crooning in a mood of subdued ecstasy till the fivefold invocation to Death tolled out like the knocks in the opening bars of the Fifth Symphony."

Nor do we need to spend much time in discussing the outward form of the poem and its main theme. There appears to be general agreement that the poem is constructed rather like an opera. It has a clearly discernible overture, followed by passages of recitative and aria. One may note, however, that the finale by no means matches the overture in symphonic complexity, being comparatively muted and, despite the richly suggestive images of the bird, the sea, and the old crone rocking the cradle, relatively downright and matter of fact in tone. The conclusion in a short recessional rather than a finale.

The main theme of "Out of the Cradle," though it does not exhaust the meanings of the poem, is the origin of the poet's genius. Whitman asks for and receives from the sea a "clew" or "word," and we are led to understand that his poetic genius originated in childhood and its first intuition of the alienation /60/ and loss which are the lot of all beings and which culminate in death. "Out of the Cradle," then, is a poem about the origin of poetry and to this extent is similar to Yeats's "Byzantium" and certain books of Wordsworth's *Prelude*. If this is not clear from the poem itself, we have as guideposts the two earlier titles Whitman gave to it: "A Child's Reminiscence" and "A Word Out of the Sea."

Is Whitman right, by the way, in tracing the origin of his poetry as he does? At best he seems to be only half right, for the world of experience posited in "Out of the Cradle" is not that of "Song of Myself," a greater poem and in many ways more characteristic of the author.

What is not so clear is how much else, if anything, the poem means. Is it, as is often said, an "organic" poem, affirming a whole view of reality in which life and death or love and death are understood as compensatory parts of the living universal rhythm? Mr. Miller, in his chapter on "Out of the Cradle," thinks that it is this kind of poem and provides us with a good statement of his position. He is speaking about the conclusion of the poem:

The sea waves, "delaying not, hurrying not," repeat their single word, "Death, death, death, death, death." The slow and funereal march of the stress ironically recalls the preceding lines of heavy, repeated stresses, lines of both joy and sorrow. The sea waves' line not only recalls but also reconciles or merges the joy with the sorrow, for the hypnotic effect ("Creeping thence steadily up to my ears and laving me softly all over") precipitates in the soul of the protagonist not terror but the ecstasy of mystic insight and affirmation. Something of the nature of that insight is sug- /61/ gested parenthetically at the end of the poem. Those sea waves striking unceasingly and rhythmically against the shore, forming the spiritually fertile "liquid rims" are "like some old crone rocking the cradle." The poem ends as it began ("Out of the cradle endlessly rocking"), and the cycle of the experience, like the cycle of life, is begun again. Life and death are not the beginning and end, but rather ceaseless continuations. Death is birth into spiritual life. The sea, as it sends its waves unceasingly to the seashore, is the " cradle endlessly rocking," just as the spiritual world, through the mystic experience of death, provides the "cradle" for man's spiritual birth.

There are many things to be said about this passage. One might start with the language and politely desire of Mr. Miller that he eschew the word "protagonist" unless the sense of the Greek word is precisely demanded. A "protagonist" combats something, but what, in "Out of the Cradle," is the "protagonist" combating? It is actually the *poet* who speaks in this poem. Then there is that other word that seems often to go with "protagonist"—"insight," the insight we and the protagonist get when the protagonist has a confrontation with something. The insight Mr. Miller attributes to the protagonist is not really an insight; it is a highly abstract idea, for which there is no warrant in the poem. Finally the word "mystic"—"the ecstasy of mystic insight and affirmation" and "the mystic experience of death." I can conceive of a mystic insight, though I would want to call it an "intuition," but an affirmation is necessarily of the will and the mystic experience requires a suspension of the will. Nor do I think much is gained by saying that the ex- /62/ perience of death in the poem is "mystic." It strikes me as being immediate and poignant; the poem would be poorer if it were not. In talking about poetry we are often tempted to use the word "mystic" in order to beg a question or to talk about something other than what we ought to be talking about: namely, the poem. I am not particularly interested in whether or not Whitman may be properly called a "mystic," because the question is so largely irrelevant to the poems. As I said in my book on Whitman:

It seems a matter of general principal that poetic experience, although it may include it, cannot be equated with or produced by mystic experience, properly so called. Mysticism leads to the ecstatic contemplation of the naught; it does not of itself produce poetry, which is a metaphorical construction of the aught. Poetry is made by the imagination, and, as Santayana insists, the life of reason depends on our ability to distinguish between the imaginative and the mystic (although he himself failed to do so in his attack on Whitman). I do not wish to deny the usefulness of the word "mysticism" in speaking of the general tenor of Whitman's mind, but only to doubt its relevance to the strictly literary question and to the question of his emergence as a poet.

My general objection to Mr. Miller's formulation occurred to me when he passed confidently by the "old crone rocking the cradle." I don't feel comfortable with that "old crone" despite her "sweet garments" (shrouds can be "sweet") and despite her cradle-rocking activities. She gives me the creeps and I can't help feeling that at not too many levels of meaning below the /63/ surface that cradle is a coffin. It is certainly true that many of Whitman's poems—including some of his best, such as "Song of Myself"—affirm an organic universe and an immortal and universal rhythm of life, but "Out of the Cradle" is not one of them. The quality of experience conveyed by this poem—the experience out of which poetry is born—involves love without an object; it involves anxiety, alienation, insoluble contradiction, and ultimate despair, a despair not assuaged by the sentimental resignation with which it is embraced.

The illusion of a harmonious universe in which opposites or contradictions are reconciled is sustained only at the very beginning of the poem. There the "musical shuttle" out of "the mocking-bird's throat" draws into a unity that which is "down" and that which is "up":

> Down from the shower'd halo,
> Up from the mystic play of shadows twining and twisting as
>   if they were alive ...

An at the beginning of the poem the poet can confidently speak of himself as the "chanter of pains and joys, uniter of here and hereafter." The feeling of reconciliation and harmony rises to an early pitch in the aria of the two birds:

> *Shine! Shine! Shine!*
> *Pour down your warmth, great sun!*
> *While we bask, we two together.*
> *Two together!*
> *Winds blow south, or winds blow north,*
> *Day come white, or night come black,*
> *Home, or rivers and mountains from home, /64/*
> *Singing all time, minding no time,*
> *While we two keep together.*

But the illusion of unity and continuity is not sustained, or is sustained only fitfully, after this aria. For now the she-bird has suddenly disappeared, and the he-bird sings his melancholy dirge, pouring out meanings, as Whitman cryptically says, "which I of all men know." A reader mindful of Whitman's love of melodrama, of which he encountered aplenty in the Italian operas he was so fond of, will find the first ominous note in this ominous poem in the "surging of the sea," for this surging is described as "hoarse," and although we may see nothing necessarily frightening in this at first, the context of the poem forces us to remember that ghosts and other demonic creatures are often said to speak with a hoarse and sepulchral voice. Even the "white arms out in the breakers tirelessly tossing" which Whitman remembers seeing during the childhood experience he is recapturing or re-creating do not seem on reflection to be so attractive and winsome as they do at first. There is something threatening, something beyond human control, something suggestive of a universe indifferent to human destiny, in that tireless tossing. Or perhaps there is something merely suggestive of death, for the arms of a corpse in the sea might toss tirelessly.

The object of love is now unattainable, though there is still the compulsion to pursue it in panic and madness, a pursuit now seen as an act of nature itself:

> *O madly the sea pushes upon the land,*
> *With love, with love.*

/65/ And whereas once the white and the black were held together in a unison,

> *Day come white, or night come black,*

they are now seen in an ultimate opposition:

> *What is that little black thing I see there in the white?*

The song of the he-bird now rises to a pitch of desperate assertion:

> *Shake out carols!*
> *Solitary here, the night's carols!*
> *Carols of lonesome love! death's carols!*
> *Carols under that lagging, yellow, waning moon!*
> *O under that moon where she droops almost down into the sea!*
> *O reckless despairing carols.*

And finally the song recedes into a resigned reminiscence of what used to be: "We two together no more."

Although we now hear "the aria sinking," "all else" continues; the stars shine, the winds blow, the notes of the bird echo. But "all else" does not continue in a compensatory or organic harmony. Instead, the world has fallen apart. There is no object for "the love in the heart long pent" even though it is "now loose, now at last tumultuously bursting." This is a world characterized by loss and alienation, not presided over by a benign Great Mother, as Whitman of all poets might have wished, but haunted and agitated by the "angry moans" of "the fierce old mother incessantly moaning." Through the fissures of a disjoined world there enter the demonic powers always drawn upon by /66/ the imagination of melodrama. Does the boy, the poet-to-be, receive comforting and joyous answers to his questions about his destiny? Far from it:

> The undertone, the savage old mother incessantly crying,
> To the boy's soul's questions sullenly timing, some drown'd secret hissing,
> To the outsetting bard.

At this point the bird is addressed as "demon or bird," and I think we are safe in taking "demon" in both of its usual meanings: the poetic genius and a sinister emanation from some unknown realm. The latter meaning is confirmed by the imagery that occurs a bit later, where the bird is called a messenger, as if from some infernal place:

> The messenger there arous'd, the fire, the sweet hell within,
> The unknown want, the destiny of me.

Perhaps it is also sustained by the later phrase "my dusky demon and brother." As I have already suggested, neither the fivefold invocation to death, the dusky demon, nor the old crone at the end of "Out of the Cradle" suggests a world stabilized in a compensatory order of life and death. If we have read the poem clearly we do not leave it confident that we live in a world of pain assuaged, contradictions reconciled, and disruptive powers placated, or that poetry originates in such a world. Despite its sentimentality, Whitman's poem is more clairvoyant and more extreme in its perception of disorder and dread than its critics have seen, although these same critics would readily discern the same qualities in the works of other American romancers, such as Cooper, Poe, Hawthorne, and Melville. /67/

Let me recall at this point the fascination Whitman felt for Poe and his writings. As he tells us in *Specimen Days,* he thinks that Poe's verses "by final judgment, probably belong among the electric lights of imaginative literature, brilliant and dazzling, but with no heat." Nevertheless, he says, there is "an indescribable magnetism" about these poems with their "incorrigible propensity toward nocturnal themes" and their "demoniac undertone behind every page." And Whitman tells us that he had gradually lost his early distaste for Poe's writings. He then recounts a dream he had had about Poe: "I saw a vessel on the sea, at midnight, in a storm . . . flying uncontrolled with torn sails and broken spars through the wild sleet and winds and waves of the night. On the deck was a slender, slight, beautiful figure, a dim man apparently enjoying all the terror, the murk, and the dislocation of which he was the centre and the victim." That makes a good description of the author of "Out of the Cradle"—a dim man apparently enjoying all the terror, the murk, and the dislocation of which he was the center and the victim.

But, it might be asked, is not my account of "Out of the Cradle" at odds with the obvious feelings the poet means to leave us with? These feelings involve sadness, to be sure, but they seem to culminate, if not in happiness, then in resignation in the face of loss and unrequited love. And death itself, it might be argued, is not felt to be terrible; indeed it is embraced with a kind of tender eroticism, not to mention gustatory delight—"the low and delicious word death." It seems to me that the language of the poem sustains these feelings of resignation and benignity so well that it is all too easy to take them as the sum and sub- /68/ stance of the poem. As D. H. Lawrence admonishes us, we must look below the surface of these American authors. When we look below the surface of "Out of the Cradle" we seem to see the dark workings-out of a human drama being played on a stage set by a dramatist with a dubious moral to propose, namely that we should accept death and that this acceptance may be the origin of such creations as Whitman's poetry. This would be excellent morality if the sense of it were: "Let us accept death as a fact, and let this fact thereby enhance our life." But Whitman does not say anything like this. He is titillated by death and he forms a sentimental attachment to it. The idyl of the two birds ends near the beginning of the poem, but the idyllic tone, modulated into a somber key, strangely continues. And in fact what the poet does is nothing less than endow the ominous drama of the savage old mother, the lagging moon, and the dusky demon with the emotional quality of an idyl; he thus successfully muffles and suffuses but cannot banish what is going on under the surface. The melodious words and the bland universe of experience make one level of the poem, but the submerged, disrupted, and ultimately nihilistic impulses remain active.

We do not have to be professional psychoanalysts in order to make the plausible conjecture that the reason for the disjunction between the manifest and the latent content of Whitman's poem is to be found in the poet's own emotional life. The generally accepted view of Whitman is that he was more or less bisexual, that he tended toward the homosexual, that he was perhaps not very active sexually at all, and that love, for him, was either fraternal or maternal—he was unable to endow a father image with emotional power or to convey, except in very abstract /69/ terms, the nature of heterosexual love. In "Out of the Cradle" the neurotic Whitman has it all his own way. There is no image of paternity: "fish-shaped" Paumonok is not identified with the father here, although it is in "As I Ebb'd with the Ocean of Life." The marriage of sexual equals is symbolically exorcised in the loss of the she-bird by the he-bird. The he-bird is not felt as a father, but as "my dusky demon and brother." In this world bereft of the father-principle, the mother is all-encompassing, like the sea. But what is the price the poet has to pay for his denial and extinction of the father? Well, of course, it is anxiety and ambivalence, involving both love and dread, toward the mother. Thus, it is not surprising that while the poet is enjoying with such swooning pleasure the rocking of the cradle, the mother supplying the motive power should be an "old crone" who "bends aside" and whispers hoarsely.

On the surface, in other words, the embracing of death is presented as pleasurable and as the beginning of creative acts. Beneath the surface it is recognized as an act of neurotic regression which generates powerful and sinister impulses that threaten the destruction of personality. This is why I speak of the "melodramatic" quality of "Out of the Cradle," apart from its obvious use of some of the trappings of this mode of art. Whitman's distinctive emotional nature is to be found in the conflicts of the unresolved Oedipus complex we all of us more or less live with (and it is here rather than in the sentimental invocation to death that we discover the real origins of Whitman's poetry—insofar as we discover them at all). Melodrama, like some forms of comedy—farce, for example—is precisely a drama of unresolved conflicts or contradictions. /70/

The poem called "Tears" is a kind of footnote to the more lachrymose sections of "Out of the Cradle." This short lyric starts out as a rather impressive piece but at the end, where we read about "the unloosen'd ocean/ Of tears! tears! tears!" it is hard not to be reminded of Alice in Wonderland, swimming in the ocean she has made with her weeping. Nevertheless the ambiguity or doubleness of "Out of the Cradle" is well represented, and in a more literal way, in "Tears." Here the poet imagines himself to be "sedate and decorous by day, with calm countenance and regulated pace." But at night he is a ghost with a "muffled head" weeping desperately on the beach:

> O who is that ghost? that form in the dark, with tears?
> What shapeless lump is that, bent, crouch'd there on the sand?
> Streaming tears, sobbing tears, throes, choked with wild cries;
> O storm, embodied, rising, careering with swift steps along the beach?
> O wild and dismal night storm, with wind . . .

There is nothing here about an "outsetting bard." There is only an undifferentiated horror and in a gothicized setting an almost total extinction of personality.

If I am right in assigning to "Out of the Cradle" such terms as romance, idyl, and melodrama, it cannot, as I have noted before, be also a tragic poem. It would be surprising indeed if a work of personal confession whose main emotions culminate, as we must see, in a sentimental nihilism should be also a tragic work. The poem does not work its way through its own inner contradictions, its *agon*, and then proceed, as does tragedy, to issue in a higher synthesis or harmony. The embracing of death /71/ is not accompanied by a purgated emotion, because the emotion is not won; it is, we cannot help feeling, merely held in reserve so that at the proper time the poet can fall back on it. It is an emotion all too easily come by, in other words a sentimental, though not a shallow, emotion. "Song of Myself" can hardly be called a tragedy either, but that poem strikes me as having more of the essential nature of tragic art than does "Out of the Cradle"—at least, "Song of Myself" has, in the correct sense of the word, a protagonist. "Out of the Cradle" is a much more unified work of art than Melville's *Pierre* (to venture a distant comparison); but it seems to me to be related to "Song of Myself" roughly as *Pierre*—also a work that begins in idyl and ends in melodrama—is related to *Moby-Dick*. After the great aggressive act of creating a superb work of art there follows, for aesthetic, moral, or psychological reasons we cannot quite define, the rather desperate act of neurotic self-exposure. The poet who in "Song of Myself" glorified in the amplitude of a many-faceted personality has come in the Sea-Drift poems to doubt the very possibility of personality. He has been led, for whatever reason, to wonder whether the glorious autonomous self has not now become (in the memorable words of Fredrik Schyberg) "only a chance bit of wreckage thrown up on the shore of existence."

The characteristic form of American fiction which I call in a special sense "romance" is one which defines itself by its substitution of two-dimensional figures, often allegorized, for the rounded characters who appear in the more ample form of the novel. It defines itself, that is, by a reduction of personality. For this reason, among the others I have pointed out, romance is a suitable form for "Out of the Cradle Endlessly Rocking."

Neil D. Isaacs

The Autoerotic Metaphor*

* * *

So far five forms of autoerotic metaphor have been seen: the explosion of a Roman Candle, the frenzied motion of riding a rocking-horse, the sensations of springs while bathing in a garden, the practicing of a fiddle, and music as feeling in general. I list them now because each has a bearing on the sixth form, Whitman's in "Out of the Cradle Endlessly Rocking," and because I doubt that I would ever have noticed autoerotism here without the prior observation of the others. /105/

"Out of the Cradle Endlessly Rocking" is a veritable Whitman's sampler of his typical themes and devices. The poet sings a reminiscence of a boyhood experience, a summer's observations of a bird who lost his mate and sang of his loss in songs which the poet now translates. But the reason the experience is important is for what it meant to the boy, not the bird.

The rocking motion is present, not only in the title and echoing verbs throughout but also in the characteristic, furiously charging rhythms. The Roman candle explodes here, too, not literally in a fireworks display, but in the last two stanzas of the bird's song with the playing out of the moon's brown halo into the sea, when the language is ecstatically punctuated with *O*'s, just as with Gerty MacDowell. Perhaps the feathered guest is playing Nausicaa to Whitman's Odysseus, with Paumanok serving as Phaeacia-Sandymount. As for the sensual touch of springs, the effect of the sea renders "the boy ecstatic, with his bare feet . . . dallying." The sea pushes madly "upon the land, / with love," the waves soothing each other, the sea "laving me softly all over."

---

* Reprinted from *Literature and Psychology*, xv (Spring 1965), 104–6, by permission.

Most important, there is the musical metaphor, but not with any instrument other than the poet's and boy's and bird's gift of song. The two lone singers, bird and boy-translator, pour forth their anguished, passionate, vainly sensual love-call. But the weight of the analogies, however heavily numerous, cannot alone impress the interpretation upon the reader. Nor is the setting absolutely convincing, however convenient the idea of an adolescent indulging in solitary expressions of love-feelings may be for the reading. It is the language itself that impressively supports the impression of autoerotism.

Gerunds (risings and fallings, yearning), present participles, prepositions (up, out, over, from, from under) are the principal parts of speech bearing the metaphorical train of thought. But I'll confine my list to some of the more suggestive idioms and bits of phrasing. For example, as the bird imagines his mate in shapes in the foam and the moon, the boy imagines "white arms out in the breakers" and the moon to be "heavy with love."

A further analogy with the Joyce episode is the tumescence-detumescence technique, suggested in such lines as "O rising stars! / Perhaps the one I want so much will rise" and "The aria sinking." Even more impressive are lines which suggest the actual physical description of autoerotism, such as "High and clear I /106/ shoot my voice over the waves," "O trembling throat," "Pierce the woods, the earth," "Shake out carols!" "The yellow half-moon enlarged, sagging down, drooping," "The love in the heart long pent, now loose, now at last tumultuously bursting," "swiftly depositing," "Some drowned secret hissing," and "O you singer solitary, singing by yourself, protecting me. / Never more the cries of unsatisfied love be absent from me."

Finally, the old orgasm-dying equation enters in, serving as a kind of incremental refrain, when at the climax of the bird's song comes "Loved! loved! loved! loved! loved!" which becomes, towards the end of the poem's detumescence, "Death, death, death, death, death."

James E. Miller, Jr.

The "Rocking Cradle" and a Reminiscence*

"Out of the Cradle Endlessly Rocking" is a vivid, imaginative re-creation by the mature poet of the primary childhood experience that determined him to be a poet and granted him poetic (or spiritual) insight. In understanding the structure of the poem it is important to note the "time" frame within which the action of the drama is set. The poet is "A man, yet by these tears a little boy again" and he is "borne hither," back to the scene of the unforgettable boyhood experience by recollection of all the images of nature that played such important roles in the experience. But in addition the poet remembers the experience so vividly because he recalls "the thousand responses of my heart never to cease," the "myriad thence-arous'd words," and "the word stronger and more delicious than any." All the poet's poems are reminders of that one crucial experience and carry him back, almost against his will. Indeed, with the onrush of all the lines of the opening section, lines tumbled onto each other by the swiftly moving "out of," "over," "down," "up from," "out from," "from," the poet is apparently overwhelmed with recollections that spring out at him from all directions at once. Possessed by an insistent memory, the poet finds himself helpless as he is transported imaginatively back into the past of his childhood. He curiously looks upon the words of this poem as somehow detached from and uncontrolled by him:

> From such as now they [the words] start the scene revisiting,
> As a flock, twittering, rising, or overhead passing.

---

* Reprinted from *A Critical Guide to Leaves of Grass* (Chicago: The University of Chicago Press, 1966), pp. 104–10, by permission.

120

The metaphor of the flock itself suggests that the poet's will has been subverted by his overpowering memory and the experience is, in a sense, forcefully re-creating itself. /105/

Although the poem in the main is the boy's experience, the reader is not allowed to forget throughout that that experience is re-created out of a man's memory, the recollection of a mature poet, and the experience has its greatest significance in relation to the man as poet. When the he-bird first discovers his mate missing and sends forth his first anguished cry, the poet confides, "He pour'd forth the meanings which I of all men know." And when the poet reveals, "I have treasur'd every note," he is suggesting to the reader that the bird's song has a significance far beyond what is apparent in the dramatic incidents of the poem. At the end of the poem, too, the poet reminds the reader that the experience of the poem is not immediate but recalled, and recalled primarily because the experience reveals the source of the mature man's poetic vision. As the bird sang to the boy "in the moonlight on Paumanok's gray beach," the song evoked, like that "flock, twittering, rising," a "thousand responsive songs at random"; the poet says simply, "My own songs awaked from that hour." In this line lies the key to the primary meaning of "Out of the Cradle Endlessly Rocking."

This frame, of the adult poet re-creating in his imagination a boyhood experience, serves not only to inclose and give form to that experience but also to endow it with its primary significance. The boy is not just an ordinary boy but an "outsetting bard." The man recalling the boy is the accomplished bard. The "meaning" of the poem, if it is to have a meaning separate from the drama, is the "meaning" of the experience for the poet's songs. What are the "meanings" that the poet "of all men" knows? Why were his songs "awaked from that hour"? Perhaps one of the secrets of the triumph of this poem is that its "meaning" is nowhere explicitly stated but is imaginatively and emotionally evoked. The reader, like the boy in the poem, lives the experience and through that experience comes intuitively to *know*.

In order to discover the meaning closest to that intended by the poet, it is perhaps best to examine closely the dramatic action of the poem. The characters of the action as well as the setting function symbolically, and the action itself becomes ultimately symbolic. There are three stages in the drama of the re-created experience. In the first the dominant characters are the two mockingbirds, the "two feather'd guests from Alabama," who in their carol of bliss sing /106/ the song of ideal love and happiness. In the second stage, introduced with the sudden disappearance of the she-bird, the male mockingbird becomes

the central character and sings his powerful, anguished lament for his
lost love, a carol of "lonesome love." In the final stage of the experience, the ocean becomes the main character and sings its song. Compared to the preceding carols, the ocean's song is barren, for it has
only one word—death. But that word is the missing "clew."

Though these "characters" successively assume center stage in the
drama, it must be remembered that what is happening is doubly seen
and heard. It is filtered first through the consciousness of the boy who
is there; it is filtered next through the memory of the boy become
man and poet. The reader is thus twice removed from the actual experience. It is this indirect point of view in the poem that constitutes
its realism. Only the brilliant imagination of the boy could translate
the music of the birds and the sound of the sea into words; only the
poet could fuse these "messages" into a profound insight into the
nature of man's fate. In reality, then, the central character throughout
is the boy, shadowing forth the man-poet he is to become, and attention is focused not on the birds and sea but on the boy-man's deepen-
ing understanding wrought by the impingement of these elements of
nature on his sensitive consciousness. Each of the stages outlined
above broadens the boy-poet's awareness of the nature of life and
death. In the first stage the protagonist learns something of the nature
of fulfilled love. While the two mockingbirds are together, they sing
"all time" and mind "no time" in their bliss; out of their transfigur-
ing love they create their own eternity. After the she-bird becomes
lost, "may-be kill'd, unknown to her mate," the protagonist gains insight into "lonesome love," a love deprived of its beloved, an anguished love of the spirit, a love that has nothing to sustain it except
the spiritual.

Finally, after the aria of the he-bird "sinks," the protagonist cries
out: "O if I am to have so much, let me have more!" And as the sea
sends forth its single word, "death," as the ocean chants the word
"death," the protagonist responds with the emotional fervor of a deep
and intuitive insight. He "fuses"

> . . . the song of my dusky demon and brother,
> That he sang to me in the moonlight on Paumanok's gray beach, /107/
> With the thousand responsive songs at random,
> My own songs awaked from that hour,
> And with them the key, the word up from the waves.

This fusion is not a fusion of logic in the intellect but rather a fusion
of the emotions in the soul. The meaning of the aria of the bird has

been "deposited" in his soul ("the ears, the soul, swiftly depositing"), and the sea's word has been a response to the "boy's soul's questions." The fusion, then, of his songs, the bird's carol, and the sea's chant is a fusion in which the soul acts as catalyst. The poetry of this "outsetting bard" is to be forever spiritually tinged with the lament of lonesome love and the "strong and delicious word," death. There is the inevitable suggestion of the spiritual fulfilment of lonesome love in death, a concept dominant in the "Calamus" poems. The sea is described as "hissing melodious" its word of death. Such a phrase, a conscious juxtaposition of words whose connotations clash, suggests the paradoxical nature of death: "hissing" connotes all the horror aroused at the thought of death; "melodious" connotes all the happiness and harmony resulting from the spiritual fulfilment of death. It is an intuitive understanding of this paradox, an insight into the relationship of death and love, death as the spiritual fulfilment of love, that is the "meaning" of the poem and that informs the "thousand responsive songs" forged in the soul of the mature poet.

But the most important elements in "Out of the Cradle Endlessly Rocking" have so far gone almost unnoticed; these are the elements that bring about or "precipitate" the protagonist's insight into love and death. Whether they are regarded as mere elements of the setting or as highly charged symbols, surely there can be no doubt that the sun and moon, the day and night, the land and sea, the stars and waves play significant roles in convincing or persuading through the logic of emotion. As least there can be no disagreement that the *poetry* of "Out of the Cradle Endlessly Rocking" exists primarily in the dramatic use of these vividly created images.

It is no accident that in the first part of the poem, when the two mockingbirds are described in their wedded bliss, Paumanok is pictured in brilliant colors. The "lilac-scent" is in the air and "Fifth-month grass" is growing. In the bird's nest among the briars are "four light-green eggs spotted with brown." Amid all this color and all /108/ these images suggestive of life, fertility, and love, the two birds together sing out their paean of joy:

> *Shine! Shine! Shine!*
> *Pour down your warmth, great sun!*
> *While we bask, we two together.*

The sun is the great life-giver, and to it the birds pay tribute for their supreme happiness. But the tone of the joint song of the birds is one of defiance—

> *Winds blow south or winds blow north,*
> *Day come white, or night come black*

—a defiance of the elements as long as the birds remain "two together."

Those very winds defied by the two birds in their song of happiness are invoked by the he-bird as he searches for his lost mate: "Blow! blow! blow!" The meter of the stark line, recalling the opening of the previous carol ("Shine! shine! shine!"), brings into dramatic focus not only the change of fortune of the singer but also the transformed setting. Instead of the sun pouring down its great warmth, now the stars glisten, the waves slap the shore, and the moonbeams intertwine with the shadows. Day has become night. Attention is gradually shifted from the land (the sea is not even mentioned in the bird's opening carol) to the ocean. And such images as "the white arms out in the breakers tirelessly tossing," suggestive of unassuageable grief, reflect the tragic turn that events have taken.

The he-bird's carol of lonesome love, which forms in more senses than one the real heart of the poem, is justly celebrated for its incomparable marriage of sound and image. The three heavy beats of the previous songs are repeated not only in the opening line ("Soothe! soothe! soothe!") but also at intervals throughout, strong reminders of the tragic transformation. As the he-bird in his song scans the ocean, the land, and the sky for any sign of his beloved, he re-creates a world after his own emotional image. The breakers and waves of the sea, the brown-yellow, sagging moon, the land, and the rising stars—all reflect the he-bird's dejected and despairing state. These objects of the setting emerge vividly as symbols. When the bird cries out—
/109/

> *O brown halo in the sky near the moon, drooping upon the sea!*
> *O troubled reflection in the sea!*

—both moon and sea are symbols. But it is well to remember that they are not functioning directly as such for the reader. The reader sees both moon and sea as the man-poet remembers, when a boy, having imagined their appearance to the grieving bird. From this circuitous route these natural objects emerge charged with complex meanings by the minds through which they have filtered. The very universe comes to reflect like a mirror the emotional turbulence disturbing the bird, the boy, and the poet.

The opening duet of bliss and the he-bird's lament introduce a series of opposites suggestive of the duality of nature: sun and moon, day and night, land and sea. These pairs indicate not only a dual but also a rhythmical universe, a universe whose patterned unfolding must be the result of some unrevealed purpose. But there is additional significance to these symbols. The sun, day, and land are associated with the blissful, fulfilled life of the birds—"two together." The moon, night, and sea are associated with unfulfilled, lonesome love, a love deprived of its object. In short, one set of these symbols is associated with physical love, the body, and life; the other with spiritual love, the soul, and death. Out of these associations comes the suggestion that life and death too, like day and night, are merely a part of the rhythmical evolution of the universe.

When the he-bird in his anguished lament cries out—

> *O madly the sea pushes upon the land,*
> *With love, with love*

—it is, surely, with some understanding of the land and sea as symbols of body and soul. The sea "loves" the land as the spirit is attracted to the body, gains its identity through the body, finds its fulfilment only through the physical. With the land and sea established as symbols of the material and spiritual (they have been established as such in earlier sections of *Leaves of Grass*), the point of contact, the shore, inevitably develops special significance. It is symbolic of death itself, that point where the material life ends and the spiritual begins. The poet has exploited this special symbolic significance by using as the setting for his drama the seashore, with the he-bird singing his lament from the land to the she-bird lost over /110/ the sea. The poet makes explicit use of this symbolic significance of the seashore near the end of the poem, when he portrays the boy as crying out for the "clew":

> Are you whispering it, and have been all the time, you sea-waves?
> Is that it from your liquid rims and wet sands?

It is the sound of the wave dashing the shore's wet sands that the boy translates into the "low and delicious word death."

The "clew," then, is provided not by the sea but rather by the seashore, by the sea and the land jointly. "Liquid rims and wet sands" vividly suggest the land and sea inextricably intermingled or, symbolically, the conjunction of the physical and the spiritual. The sea waves, "delaying not, hurrying not," repeat their single word, "Death, death, death, death, death." The slow and funereal march of the stress ironically recalls the preceding lines of repeated heavy stresses, lines of both joy and sorrow. The sea waves' line not only recalls but also reconciles or merges the joy with the sorrow, for the hypnotic effect ("Creeping thence steadily up to my ears and laving me softly all over") precipitates in the soul of the protagonist not terror but the ecstasy of mystic insight and affirmation. Something of the nature of that insight is suggested parenthetically at the end of the poem. Those sea waves striking unceasingly and rhythmically against the shore, forming the spiritually fertile "liquid rims," are "like some old crone rocking the cradle." The poem ends as it began ("Out of the cradle endlessly rocking"), and the cycle of the experience, like the cycle of life, is begun again. Life and death are not the beginning and end, but rather ceaseless continuations. Death is birth into spiritual life. The sea, as it sends its waves unceasingly to the seashore, is the "cradle endlessly rocking," just as the spiritual world, through the mystic experience of death, provides the "cradle" for man's spiritual birth.

Edwin H. Miller

The Low and Delicious
Word *Death**

Attempts to find the origin of "Out of the Cradle Endlessly Rocking" in a personal experience about 1858 or 1859 strike me as mis-
guided and irrelevant, since the significance of an unsuccessful love
affair (if one could be proved) would be not so much the event itself
as the reactivation of the experience of loss, ultimately the loss of the
beloved mother, Whitman always, as observed earlier, intuitively
arriving at a profound psychological insight. (If one must seek a
specific event, I suggest, once again, that the death of his father in
1855 cannot be overlooked: it is perhaps more than coincidental that
only after his death does the poet meditate upon the subject, and
that reconciliation with death may be part of his reconciliation with
the father.) Thus Bychowski's explanation comes closest to describing the affect of the poem:

> When we reduce the poignant beauty of this poem to its unconscious
> core, we see the first separation of infancy, the first anguish of infantile
> love underlying all the future pain of love. Sweet death emerges then as
> the great benefactor, as a supreme salvation, since it promises a reunion
> with the beloved mother, earth, sea, and maybe the universe.

Influenced by the fact that the bird's song is called an "aria," critics
have likened the "trio"—the male bird that has lost its mate, the sea,
and the boy-poet—to the Italian opera which Whitman attended and
admired most of his life. The analogy is misleading, since, except for
the "aria," the poem does not contain the set pieces and brilliant
virtuosity of Donizetti and Bellini. In an anonymous defense of the

---

* Reprinted from *Walt Whitman's Poetry: A Psychological Journey*, pp. 175–86.
Copyright © 1968 by Edwin Haviland Miller, by permission of the publisher,
Houghton Mifflin Company.

poem shortly after its publication, Whitman himself carefully refrains from stressing the operatic qualities of the bird's "aria": "the purport of this wild and plaintive song, well-enveloped, and eluding definition, is positive and unquestionable, like the effect of music"—an explanation which, to say the least, explains little.*

Although a few of Whitman's friends, as he reported to Horace Traubel in 1888, said that "Wagner is Leaves of Grass done into music," the poet's initial response to the comparison was "adverse, critical." He was apparently troubled that Wagner, according to rumor, was not a democrat, that his "art was distinctly the art of caste," and that his "Jack and the Beanstalk stories" were unsuitable to "this modern medium." The poet had to "confess that I have heard bits here and there at concerts, from orchestras, bands, /176/ which have astonished, ravished me, like the discovery of a new world." Mostly on the basis of the enthusiasm of his friends, Whitman came to the conclusion, in 1889, that Wagner's operas "are constructed on my lines—attach themselves to the same theories of art that have been responsible for Leaves of Grass."

Although the poet and his admirers finally agreed on the question, neither condescended to specificity in indicating the artistic and thematic bonds between the two artists. In one of the most perceptive discussions of Whitman's poem, Leo Spitzer points to the coincidence (also noted by Bychowski) of the appearance in 1857 of *Tristan und Isolde* and in 1859 of "A Child's Reminiscence" (the original title). Noting the "Wagnerian orchestration," Spitzer terms the rhyming participial forms a *leitmotif* and observes in both artists "the same feeling for the voluptuousness of death and the death-like quality of love." Spitzer's insights are suggestive rather than developed, perhaps because he is primarily interested in establishing "Out of the Cradle Endlessly Rocking" as a modern elaboration upon the ancient ode.

Unlike Italian opera, "Out of the Cradle Endlessly Rocking" is an introspective "portrait of the artist as a young man," a very personal meditation which is not given a conventional public form for the obvious reason that the subject matter demands a form and a rhythm consonant with its evocation of psychic depths and infantile trauma. From the opening line—in the earlier version, "Out of the rocked cradle"—technique mirrors meaning and sound mirrors sense in a fusion such as few artists have achieved. The musical equivalent of the literal motion of the cradle is the rocking quality of the crescendos and decrescendos, the ecstatic fortissimos and "laving" pianissimos,

---

* But see Whitman's statement on p. 26. [Ed.]

with their human counterparts in the emotional state of the bird and, more particularly, of the youth. To the final line, "The sea whispered me," which counteracts the despair of "The aria sinking," the poem rocks, not only through the use of *-ing* forms or recurring images like the moon, but also in the rising and falling sounds of the bird's grief and disappointed hopes, the birth imagery ("Out of the boy's mother's womb"), the comfort and loss of the mother's breast, the literal movements of the moon and the waves, the boy's transformation from despondency to an "extatic" state, and the life-journey itself, from the cradle to the coffin.

Unlike, for example, Thomas Mann, who laboriously and self-consciously approximates the Wagnerian texture and density in /177/ his prose, Whitman rarely calls attention to his artistic trickery, although his poem is an intricately woven fabric. More important, Whitman does not make suspect the emotionality inherent in the *leitmotif* by recourse to Mann's defensive and evasive irony. Whitman's sound, like Wagner's, completely expresses content or idea, for neither is plagued by an unresolved (or unresolvable) battle between mind and heart, meaning and feeling. Read aloud—and the poem, like music, refuses to remain silent on the printed page —without the intrusion of a rational mind decreeing sense or a critical intelligence attempting explication, "Out of the Cradle Endlessly Rocking" interprets itself. The erotic sounds and movements, as in Wagner's music, evoke birth, love, loss, and death.

Whitman's poem is a reminiscence of an event in the protagonist's boyhood, when on a September night he wanders along the ocean shore and hears the song of a male mockingbird lamenting the disappearance of his mate, against the (seemingly) agitated music of waves advancing and retreating, not unlike the motions of a cradle. As in "The Sleepers," this is a nighttime experience, here played out beneath an autumnal moon. The fall is the dying season of the year, which harmonizes with the bird's loss of his beloved and with the "aria sinking," but also the time of harvest and of ancient fertility rites, which harmonizes with the "death" of a boy and the birth of a boy-poet. The bird, consumed by his grief, is estranged from his environment. The emergent artist, on the other hand, finds the "key," or underlying unity, which links the grief-stricken bird, "the hoarse surging of the sea," and the youthful observer—death, life, and art.

Although Whitman no doubt observed, as he walked the beaches of Long Island in his youth, the nesting habits of birds—perhaps even those of mockingbirds from Alabama—surely his means of depicting universal loss had unconscious and cultural orgins. Elsewhere in his poetry, in "The Sleepers," for instance, he disguises and artistically distances the personal note and anguish through projection—a point he makes himself when he says of the bird, "O you demon, singing by yourself—projecting me." The he-bird ("my brother")—not the boy-poet—directly experiences man's fate, abandonment by woman (mother). For the she-bird mysteriously abandons the eggs in her nest, as the mother appears to abandon the child when other offspring arrive, or when the mother appears to permit the father to supplant the child in her affections. /178/

In view of the folklore which "explains" biological realities through tales of the stork, part of the charm of the poem is the simple fact that the child-poet begins to learn about life by observing the habits of birds, but, like all children, arrives at understanding only when he experiences another loss—the abandonment of cultural "lies." The not-so-simple fact about the poem, if we accept Freud's brilliant speculations about the boyhood of Leonardo da Vinci, is that the bird analogy, with its ancient association of the winged phallus, not only accounts for the orgiastic rhythm of the poem, but also harmonizes with the erotic nature of knowledge itself, which is expressed in the boy's longing to be "the outsetting bard of love" and in the mature man's sublimation in his art of "the cries of unsatisfied love." (Like Picasso, Whitman invariably dramatizes art in sexual terms.) With subtlety and insight Whitman remains faithful to the human drama of childhood and maturity, even to the substitution of the artistic lie for the cultural lie: the poem, on all levels, depicts rejection and ultimate reconciliation.

The "trio," as Chase observes, more than hints that the event is a veiled reenactment of the oedipal conflict, the female bird seemingly returning as "the fierce old mother," the sea, that threatens but eventually soothes when the boy begins to comprehend the "life rhythm." The male bird is both "brother" and "dusky demon," child and father. Significantly—and how accurate Whitman's language is! —the boy-poet is "Cautiously peering, absorbing, translating." Timidly, because of the complex nature of the emotional conflict, the youth observes from a safe distance, ingests literally and symbolically —"from the nipples of her breasts" in the third line (omitted in 1867) to the return to the universal mother depicted in the concluding lines—and then orders the experience artistically. Since the he-bird, like the males in "The Sleepers" and "As I Ebb'd with the Ocean of Life," is impotent in his grief, the boy in Whitmanesque fashion must discover the "key"—that is, the eternal erotic principle —without external assistance, paternal or historical.

The child, like the bird, at first knows only love, the mother bending over him in the cradle in an edenic relationship, and complacently thinks that "we two together" will always be together, that all nature conspires to insure the permanence of this idyllic relationship. /179/

> Shine! Shine!
> Pour down your warmth, great Sun!
> While we bask—we two together.
>
> Two together!
> Winds blow South, or winds blow North,
> Day come white, or night come black,
> Home, or rivers and mountains from home,
> Singing all time, minding no time,
> If we two but keep together.

The ominous words "Till of a sudden" introduce the bird to the pain and riddle of separation or loss. For the she-bird unaccountably abandons her nest and her "four light-green eggs, spotted with brown." The bird, suddenly in a new world devoid of pleasure and love, refuses to accept the finality of the situation. He breaks out into a lament in which he cries, like a child, for consolation— "Soothe! Soothe!"—but the waves, the stars, and the moon return no answer. And eventually, his voice echoing in what appears to him a waste land, he moans:

> Loved! Loved! Loved! Loved! Loved!
> Loved—but no more with me,
> We two together no more.

The moon is "sinking" on the horizon, the sound of his voice is "sinking," and his confidence is gone.

One of the most glowing descriptions of the bird's "aria" is that of John Cowper Powys in *Visions and Revisions:*

The most devastating love-cry ever uttered, except that of King David over his friend, is the cry this American poet dares to put into the heart of "a wild-bird from Alabama" that has lost its mate. I wonder if critics have done justice to the incredible genius of this man who can find words for that aching of the soul we do not confess even to our dearest?

But Powys' praise, inadvertently, does an injustice to Whitman's poem since he removes the song from its context and overemphasizes the (negative) "aching of the soul." Although the bird's loss is also the boy's loss, this is not a poem of self-pity but of a /180/ developing consciousness. And so the rocking participles in the passage immediately following—

> The aria sinking,
> All else continuing—the stars shining,
> The winds blowing—the notes of the wondrous bird echoing,
> With angry moans the fierce old mother yet, as ever, incessantly moaning,
> On the sands of Paumonok's shore gray and rustling—

reintroduce the movement of the cradle: life is endless motion. The poem itself, organically, reflects this motion, as Mrs. Dalloway's* needles duplicate the movement of the waves, and the boy's consciousness moves beyond empathy (or stasis) to awareness. As the song dies away, an artist is born.

The imagery of the poem is unobstrusively but intricately related to the exposition of the bird's despair and the boy's awakening. The moon, introduced in the eleventh line, moves across the heaven, rising and falling according to its rhythm, and, like Wagner's restless and orgiastic musical patterns, reflects the emotional tensions of the participants: "From under that yellow half-moon, late-risen, and swollen as if with tears." (Subsequently we read, "by these tears a little boy again"; "Sat the lone singer [the bird], wonderful, causing tears"; and of "the boy extatic," "The strange tears down the cheeks coursing.") In a long aria the male bird four times associates himself and his loss with the moon:

> Low hangs the moon—it rose late,
> O it is lagging—O I think it is heavy with love.
>
> .   .   .   .
>
> Low-hanging moon!
> What is that dusky spot in your brown yellow?
> O it is the shape of my mate!
> O moon, do not keep her from me any longer.
>
> .   .   .   .
>
> Carols of lonesome love! Death's carols!
> Carols under that lagging, yellow, waning moon!
> O, under that moon, where she droops almost down into the sea! /181/
>
> .   .   .   .
>
> O brown halo in the sky, near the moon, drooping upon the sea!
> O troubled reflection in the sea!

---

* The reference here is probably to Mrs. Ramsey in *To the Lighthouse*. [Ed.]

Not only do the bird and the moon appear to droop simultaneously, but also darkness appears to settle over the world. But this is the bird's reality, not that of the almost forgotten youth who has been observing and listening on the "sands of Paumanok's shore," under the same moon and in the same shadows. Unlike the bird fixated in his grief and physically and emotionally arrested on a lonely perch—

> All night long, on the prong of a moss-scallop'd stake,
> Down, almost amid the slapping waves,
> Sat the lone singer, wonderful, causing tears—

the lad is about to experience a miraculous transformation which will lead him to a reality beyond the bird's comprehension.

> The yellow half-moon, enlarged, sagging down, drooping, the face
>   of the sea almost touching,
> The boy extatic—with his bare feet the waves, with his hair the
>   atmosphere dallying,
> The love in the heart pent, now loose, now at last tumultuously
>   bursting. . . .

The erotic and birth images, as in "There Was a Child Went Forth," appropriately characterize the metamorphosis. "Extatic" is a most expressive (Whitman would say "delicious") word to describe the adventure which is both intellectual and orgiastic. For the boy knows, as the bird does not, that the setting (or dying) moon will rise again on the morrow, but on a deeper level he *senses* that the moon's erotic union with the ocean—"the face of the sea almost touching"—is part of "the procreant urge." The falling and rising of the tides, the erotic rhythm of the universe, he *senses*, contain an insight beyond that of the bird's tragic perspective, which projects its loss or betrayal upon the cosmos.

At this point the "extatic" youth's insight is limited and amorphous. In sharing the bird's grief, the boy, symbolically, enters into a brotherhood and acknowledges the universal loss upon which /182/ life rests: he has, in short, accepted "things as they are," which will be the subject matter of his art.

> Bird! (then said the boy's Soul,)
> It is indeed toward your mate you sing? or is it mostly to
>   me?
> For I that was a child, my tongue's use sleeping,

> Now that I have heard you,
> Now in a moment I know what I am for—I awake,
> And already a thousand singers—a thousand songs, clearer,
>   louder, more sorrowful than yours,
> A thousand warbling echoes have started to life within me,
> Never to die.

But the vision or illumination which will enable the artist to reconcile disparities and to rediscover the eternal order does not come at once, because the third member of the trio—the sea—has not spoken, although it has been sounding ceaselessly in the background as the bird voices its grief and as the boy is transformed into a poet.

The youth seems about to duplicate the bird's experience, the delights of "Two together" and then insurmountable grief: since he, unlike the bird, has the ability to generalize, he imagines that the "destination" of man may be universal "chaos":

> O give me some clew!
> O if I am to have so much, let me have more!
> O a word! O what is my destination?
> O I fear it is henceforth chaos!
> O how joys, dreads, convolutions, human shapes, and all shapes,
>   spring as from graves around me!
> O phantoms! you cover all the land, and all the sea!
> O I cannot see in the dimness whether you smile or frown upon
>   me;
> O vapor, a look, a word! O well-beloved!
> O you dear women's and men's phantoms!

(All but the first two lines disappeared in the revised version of 1881, when, as was his practice later in life, Whitman smoothed out the tensions in his earlier poems.) Now, for the first time, the boy listens to the "whispering" of the sea: "Is that it from your liquid rims and wet sands?"

Thus at last the sea emerges, literally and artistically, as the most powerful member of the "trio" around whom the action revolves. /183/ It voices no words, but its unuttered sounds speak as the bird's song cannot. It never alters its endless motions, which are variously viewed as invasions or embraces of the shore, depending upon the observer's predisposition, but gradually it envelops the boy-poet and the bird as the mother envelops her offspring. For the sea is eternal woman, the bird's mate as well as the mother introduced in the opening lines of the poem—

> Out of the rocked cradle,
> Out of the mocking-bird's throat, the musical shuttle,
> Out of the boy's mother's womb, and from the nipples of her breasts—

at the beginning of what Spitzer felicitously calls an " 'oceanic' sentence." The time-burdened cradle has its timeless counterpart in the motions of the waves. The event recorded in "Out of the Cradle Endlessly Rocking" occurs along Paumanok's shore, but the event that is life begins in the amniotic waters and culminates in the grave, only to repeat itself time without end.

After the she-bird's disappearance, when grief pervades and colors the atmosphere, the protagonist refers casually to "the hoarse surging of the sea" and to "slapping waves"—obliquely attributing disaster to the terrifying sea, particularly in one graphic picture of loss, "The white arms out in the breakers tirelessly tossing." But, as it turns out, the "white arms" will eventually soothe and heal the pain. In the "aria" the bird looks across the dark waters in search of his beloved and even imagines that he hears her voice above the "husky-noised sea," which, of course, is only the echo of his own lonely voice. (However, "A thousand warbling echoes have started to life within me.") The sea as a character in the dramatic action is not directly present until the bird's song is over—

> The colloquy there—the trio—each uttering,
> The undertone—the savage old mother, incessantly crying,
> To the boy's Soul's questions sullenly timing—some drowned
>   secret hissing,
> To the outsetting bard of love.

Caught up in the bird's tragedy, the emergent artist equates the bird's song and the sound of the sea: "With angry moans the fierce /184/ old mother yet, as ever, incessantly moaning." The "moaning," however, is the bird's as well as the boy's empathetic response. "Fierce old mother" is projection of uncomprehended despair upon the ocean, or eternal mother—an unsatisfactory handling of the universal loss upon which the poem is predicated.

As the lad seeks "some clew," the sea loses its fierceness and reintroduces the enveloping mother in a remarkable stanza.

> Answering, the sea,
> Delaying not, hurrying not,
> Whispered me through the night, and very plainly before
>   daybreak,

> Lisped to me constantly the low and delicious word DEATH,
> And again Death—ever Death, Death, Death,
> Hissing melodious, neither like the bird, nor like my aroused
>   child's heart,
> But edging near, as privately for me, rustling at my feet,
> And creeping thence steadily up to my ears,
> Death, Death, Death, Death, Death.

The wonderful dactyls in the first two lines, reminiscent of those at the opening of the poem, quietly prepare us for the inevitable resolution. "Lisped" is extraordinarily right in the context: it is both sound as dimly understood by a child in a mother's embrace and imitative vocalization of a child learning to make sounds, "my tongue's use sleeping." The sound or word is delicious as is any sound in an affection context where the intonation of love speaks with a clarity rarely given to uttered syllables. The sound of the word, like the waves, engulfs the boy-poet—"edging near," "rustling at my feet," "creeping." The bird's song was intellectually compre-hended: "The aria's meaning, the ears, the Soul, swiftly depositing"—but the water physically and emotionally is like the all-inclusive embrace of the mother: "And creeping thence steadily up to my ears." And the five-times repeated word rocks like the cradle itself.

As the boy-poet, who has absorbed the plight of "my brother," and the ocean become one, life (bird), art (boy), and immortality (sea) are a trio or a trinity that is one. The fertility rite beneath the autumnal moon is completed—"the key, the word up from the waves." Mythically, the artist, like Aphrodite and Everyman, spring from the water. And the rhythm of the poem (and of life) rises and falls, until the joyous but subdued decrescendo in the /185/ final line—uttered with the quiet triumph and contented satisfaction of the child-man in the arms of the eternal mother.

> Which I do not forget,
> But fuse the song of two together,
> That was sung to me in the moonlight in Paumanok's gray beach,
> With the thousand responsive songs, at random,
> My own songs, awaked from that hour,
> And with them the key, the word up from the waves,
> The word of the sweetest song, and all songs,
> That strong and delicious word which, creeping to my feet,
> The sea whispered me.

Whicher observes that the sea offers "no consoling revelations but simply reality. . . . The outsetting bard of love will be the bard of unsatisfied love because there is no other kind." But Whitman's music refutes Whicher's reading: the "delicious word" *sounds* its consolation. As the poem makes clear in the story of the birds and as the "Calamus" poems prove, "cries of unsatisfied love" characterize the poet's and man's lot, but "Out of the Cradle Endlessly Rocking" is, to quote D. H. Lawrence, "the perfect utterance of a concentrated, spontaneous soul," in which the poet endeavors to place thwarted love and death in perspective and to create a meaningful artifact and a meaningful life out of universal psychic loss. The body, life itself, and art, Whitman asserts, can be free only when death is acknowledged. Without recourse to God or mysticism, Whitman fuses, as psychologists were to do, Eros and Thanatos, repudiates the stasis of romantic despair or pessimism, and celebrates the eternal human comedy.

Structurally, the restless "oceanic" opening sentence finds rest in the quiet final line. Psychologically, the mature man has reaffirmed his faith in his artistic powers by this return to childhood experience, the source of his art (and all art) and the source of the pain which he will transcend in his intellectual-emotional insight and in creative sublimation. Finally, "Out of the Cradle Endlessly Rocking" provides an artistic and human catharsis: the poem evokes pain as we read but at the same time makes the pain endurable because it offers a metaphorical and psychological order. It moves us viscerally and emotionally when it traverses psychic depths, but consoles because we assert our humanity, not in vicarious admiration of great deeds performed by tragic heroes, /186/ which few of us will have occasion to emulate, but in the realization that the great and the mediocre can live creatively if they accept the "life rhythm. . . ."

Suggestions for Papers

Short Papers

Whitman's principal aim in his poetry was not only to reach his audience but to inspire them to an awareness of their own potential. Considering this and the fact that Whitman first presented "Out of the Cradle" to the public as a "present to them," write of your own response to the reading of either version of the poem.

Compare the basic changes in the final version of the poem and discuss their substantive function.

Challenge any of the above criticisms on the poem on the basis of your own reading experience and understanding of it.

Compare and contrast the interpretations of the poem by Griffith and Pearce.

Explore the literary references cited by Spitzer and test your findings against the use he makes of them in his approach to the poem.

Compare Whitman's attitude toward death in the final version of "Out of the Cradle" with that expressed in "When Lilacs Last in the Dooryard Bloom'd."

Compare the thematic and symbolic uses of the "bird" in either version of this poem with that of the "bird" in "When Lilacs Last in the Dooryard Bloom'd."

Discuss the meaning for you of Whitman's describing his poem as a "curious warble" the purpose of which "only comes forth, as from recesses, by many repetitions."

Choose an essay that seems to you to offer the most convincing reading of the poem and discuss why this is so.

Discuss Whitman's use of the periodic sentence, especially at the poem's beginning, as a rhetorical device to structure his free verse.

Consider his use of parallelism for a similar purpose, the effects of repetition and internal rhyme.

Is "Out of the Cradle" primarily a poem about an experience or of how an experience becomes a poem?

Discuss the question that Whitman raised in his response to the review in the *Cincinnati Commercial*. See the first paragraph in "All About a Mockingbird."

Support or take issue with the review, "Walt Whitman's New Poem."

Examine the poem closely for evidences of symbolic pairings, such as love and loss, unity and separation, the known and unknown, and discuss how Whitman attempts to reconcile them in the poem.

Longer Papers

Compare the post 1955 critics' analyses of "Out of the Cradle."

Study carefully any one of the longer explications and apply the method to another poem by Whitman, "As I Ebb'd With the Ocean of Life," "When Lilacs Last in the Dooryard Bloom'd," or "Crossing Brooklyn Ferry."

Compare a poem by Whitman with a poem by another writer of free verse, such as Carl Sandburg or William Carlos Williams.

Check the cited bibliographies for other articles on "Out of the Cradle" and write brief summaries on them in which you show how and in what ways they differ from those in this collection.

Study the cluster of poems under the title "Sea-Drift" in any complete collection of *Leaves of Grass* and define the controlling center that explains their being grouped together.

Read Emerson's essay on "The Poet" and bringing its particular points to bear on "Out of the Cradle," discuss to what extent Whitman is the answer to Emerson's call for an American poet.

In an essay on Whitman in which he refers to the poet's works as "the poetry of barbarism," George Santayana says that he "speaks to those minds and to those moods in which sensuality is touched with mysticism." Look up that essay in his book *Interpretations of Poetry and Religion*, compare it with Lawrence's essay on Whitman in *Studies in Classic American Literature* and your own response to Whitman.

Additional Readings

Bibliographies

Allen, Gay Wilson. *Walt Whitman Handbook*. Chicago: Packard and Company, 1946.

_____. *Walt Whitman as Man, Poet, and Legend: With a Check List of Whitman Publications, 1945–1960*, by Evie Allison Allen. Carbondale: Southern Illinois University Press, 1961.

Thorp, Willard. "Walt Whitman," in *Eight American Authors: A Review of Research and Criticism*, ed. Floyd Stovall. New York: W. W. Norton & Company Inc., 1963.

For the current Whitman bibliography check the quarterly *Walt Whitman Review, American Literature*, and the annual bibliography in PMLA.

Biographical, Critical, and Scholarly Studies

Allen, Gay Wilson. *American Prosody*. New York: American Book Co., 1935.

_____. *The Solitary Singer: A Critical Biography of Walt Whitman*. New York: Macmillan, 1955.

_____, (ed.) *Walt Whitman Abroad*. Syracuse: Syracuse University Press, 1955.

Asselineau, Roger. *The Evolution of Walt Whitman*. Vol. 2. Translated by the author assisted by Burton L. Cooper. Cambridge, Mass.: Harvard University Press, 1962.

Bradley, Scully. "The Fundamental Metrical Principles of Whitman's Poetry," *American Literature*, x (January, 1939), 437–59.

Brooks, Van Wyck. *The Times of Melville and Whitman*. New York: E. P. Dutton, 1947.

Chase, Richard. *Walt Whitman Reconsidered*. New York: Sloane, 1955.

De Selincourt, Basil. *Walt Whitman, a Critical Study*. London: M. Secker, 1914.

Feidelson, Charles, Jr. *Symbolism and American Literature*. Chicago: University of Chicago Press, 1953.

Fussell, Paul, Jr. "Whitman's Curious Warble: Reminiscence and Reconciliation," *The Presence of Whitman*. Edited by R. W. B. Lewis. New York: Columbia University Press, 1962.

Lawrence, D. H. *Studies in Classic American Literature*. New York: Doubleday, 1951.

Matthiessen, F. O. *American Renaissance*. New York: Oxford University Press, 1941.

Miller, James E. Jr., Karl Shapiro, and Berenice Slote. *Start with the Sun: A Study in Cosmic Poetry*. Lincoln: University of Nebraska Press, 1960.

Oliver, Egbert S. *Studies in American Literature: Whitman, Emerson, Melville & Others*. New Delhi: Eurasia Pub., 1965.

Pearce, Roy Harvey. *The Continuity of American Poetry*. New Jersey: Princeton University Press, 1961.

_____. *Whitman, a Collection of Critical Essays*. New Jersey: Prentice Hall, 1962.

Poulet, Georges. *Studies in Human Time*. Translated by Elliott Coleman. Baltimore: Johns Hopkins Press, 1956.

Symonds, John Addington. *Walt Whitman, a Study*. London, 1893.

Waskow, Howard J. *Whitman: Explorations in Form*. Chicago: The University of Chicago Press, 1966.

Whitman, Walt. *A Child's Reminiscence*. Edited by Thomas O. Mobbott and Rollo G. Silver. Seattle: University of Washington Book Store, 1930.

_____. *The Collected Writings of Walt Whitman*. Edited by Gay Wilson Allen and Sculley Bradley. 15 vols. New York: New York University Press, 1961–.

_____. *The Correspondence*. Edited by Edwin Haviland Miller. 4 vols. New York: New York University Press, 1961–.

_____. *Leaves of Grass*. Facsimile Edition 1860 text with introduction by Roy Harvey Pearce. Ithaca, N. Y.: Great Seal Books, 1961.

_____. *Whitman's Manuscripts, Leaves of Grass (1860)*. Edited by Fredson Bowers. Chicago: University of Chicago Press, 1955.

_____. *Walt Whitman's Blue Book*. The 1860–61 *Leaves of Grass* containing His Manuscript Additions and Revisions. Facsimile of the unique copy in the Oscar Lion Collection of The New York Public Library, Vol. I. Vol. 2, Textual analysis by Arthur Golden. New York: The New York Public Library, Astor, Lenox and Tilden Foundations, 1968.

General Instructions
for a Research Paper

If your instructor gives you any specific directions about the format of your research paper that differ from the directions given here, you are, of course, to follow his directions. Otherwise, you can observe these directions with the confidence that they represent fairly standard conventions.

A research paper represents a student's synthesis of his reading in a number of primary and secondary works, with an indication, in footnotes, of the source of quotations used in the paper or of facts cited in paraphrased material. A *primary* source is the text of a work as it issued from the pen of the author or some document contemporary with the work. The following, for instance, would be considered primary sources: a manuscript copy of the work; first editions of the work and any subsequent editions authorized by the writer; a modern scholarly edition of the text; an author's comment about his work in letters, memoirs, diaries, journals, or periodicals; published comments on the work by the author's contemporaries. A *secondary* source would be any interpretation, explication, or evaluation of the work printed, usually several years after the author's death, in critical articles and books, in literary histories, and in biographies of the author. In this casebook, the text of the work, any variant versions of it, any commentary on the work by the author himself or his contemporaries may be considered as primary sources; the editor's Introduction, the articles from journals, and the excerpts from books are to be considered secondary sources. The paper that you eventually write will become a secondary source.

Plagiarism

The cardinal sin in the academic community is plagiarism. The rankest form of plagiarism is the verbatim reproduction of someone else's words without any indication that the passage is a quotation. A lesser but still serious form of plagiarism is to report, in your own words, the fruits of someone else's research without acknowledging the source of your information or interpretation.

You can take this as an inflexible rule: every verbatim quotation in your paper must be either enclosed in quotation marks or single-spaced and inset from the left-hand margin and must be followed by a footnote number. Students who merely change a few words or phrases in a quotation and present the passage as their own work are still guilty of plagiarism. Passages of genuine paraphrase must be footnoted too if the information or idea or interpretation contained in the paraphrase cannot be presumed to be known by ordinary educated people or at least by readers who would be interested in the subject you are writing about.

The penalties for plagiarism are usually very severe. Don't run the risk of a failing grade on the paper or even of a failing grade in the course.

Lead-Ins

Provide a lead-in for all quotations. Failure to do so results in a serious breakdown in coherence. The lead-in should at least name the person who is being quoted. The ideal lead-in, however, is one that not only names the person but indicates the pertinence of the quotation.

Examples:

(typical lead-in for a single-spaced, inset quotation)

```
Irving Babbitt makes this observation about
Flaubert's attitude toward women:
```

(typical lead-in for quotation worked into the frame of one's sentence)

```
Thus the poet sets out to show how the present
age, as George Anderson puts it, "negates the
values of the earlier revolution."⁷
```

Full Names

The first time you mention anyone in a paper give the full name of the person. Subsequently you may refer to him by his last name.

Examples: First allusion—Ronald S. Crane

Subsequent allusions—Professor Crane, as Crane says.

Ellipses

Lacunae in a direct quotation are indicated with *three spaced periods,* in addition to whatever punctuation mark was in the text at the point where you truncated the quotation. *Hit the space-bar of your typewriter between each period.* Usually there is no need to put the ellipsis-periods at the beginning or the end of a quotation.

Example: "The poets were not striving to communi-
cate with their audience ; . . . By and
large, the Romantics were seeking . . .
to express their unique personalities."[8]

Brackets

Brackets are used to enclose any material interpolated into a direct quotation. The abbreviation *sic,* enclosed in brackets, indicates that the error of spelling, grammar, or fact in a direct quotation has been copied as it was in the source being quoted. If your typewriter does not have special keys for brackets, draw the brackets neatly with a pen.

Examples: "He [Theodore Baum] maintained that Con-
fucianism [the primary element in Chinese
philosophy] aimed at teaching each individual to accept his lot in life."[12]

"Paul Revear [sic] made his historic ride
on April 18, 1875 [sic]."[15]

Summary Footnote

A footnote number at the end of a sentence which is not enclosed in quotation marks indicates that only *that* sentence is being documented in the footnote. If you want to indicate that the footnote documents more than one sentence, put a footnote number at the end of the *first* sentence of the paraphrased passage and use some formula like this in the footnote:

[16]For the information presented in this and the
following paragraph, I am indebted to Marvin
Magalaner, Time of Apprenticeship: the Fiction of
Young James Joyce (London, 1959), pp. 81-93.

Citing the Edition

The edition of the author's work being used in a paper should always be cited in the first footnote that documents a quotation from that work. You can obviate the need for subsequent footnotes to that edition by using some formula like this:

[4]Nathaniel Hawthorne, "Young Goodman Brown," as
printed in Young Goodman Brown, ed. Thomas E.

Connolly, Charles E. Merrill Literary Casebooks
(Columbus, Ohio, 1968), pp. 3-15. This edition will
be used throughout the paper, and hereafter all
quotations from this book will be documented with a
page-number in parentheses at the end of the
quotation.

Notetaking

Although all the material you use in your paper may be contained in this
casebook, you will find it easier to organize your paper if you work from
notes written on 3 x 5 or 4 x 6 cards. Besides, you should get practice in the
kind of notetaking you will have to do for other term-papers, when you will
have to work from books and articles in, or on loan from, the library.

An ideal note is a self-contained note — one which has all the information
you would need if you used anything from that note in your paper. A note
will be self-contained if it carries the following information:

(1) The information or quotation *accurately* copied.

(2) Some system for distinguishing direct quotation from paraphrase.

(3) All the bibliographical information necessary for documenting that
note — full name of the author, title, volume number (if any), place
of publication, publisher, publication date, page numbers.

(4) If a question covered more than one page in the source, the note-card
should indicate which part of the quotation occurred on one page and
which part occurred on the next page. The easiest way to do this is
to put the next page number in parentheses after the last word on
one page and before the first word on the next page.

In short, your note should be so complete that you would never have to go
back to the original source to gather any piece of information about that note.

Footnote Forms

The footnote forms used here follow the conventions set forth in the
MLA Style Sheet, Revised Edition, ed. William Riley Parker, which is now
used by more than 100 journals and more than thirty university presses in
the United States. Copies of this pamphlet can be purchased for fifty cents
from your university bookstore or from the Modern Language Association,
62 Fifth Avenue, New York, New York 10011. If your teacher or your
institution prescribes a modified form of this footnoting system, you should,
of course, follow that system.

A primary footnote, the form used the first time a source is cited, supplies
four pieces of information: (1) author's name, (2) title of the source,

(3) publication information, (4) specific location in the source of the information or quotation. A secondary footnote is the shorthand form of documentation after the source has been cited in full the first time.

Your instructor may permit you to put all your footnotes on separate pages at the end of your paper. But he may want to give you practice in putting footnotes at the bottom of the page. Whether the footnotes are put at the end of the paper or at the bottom of the page, they should observe this format of spacing: (1) the first line of each footnote should be indented, usually the same number of spaces as your paragraph indentations; (2) all subsequent lines of the footnote should start at the lefthand margin; (3) there should be single-spacing within each footnote and double-spacing between each footnote.

Example:

¹⁰Ruth Wallerstein, <u>Richard</u> <u>Crashaw</u>: <u>A</u> <u>Study</u> <u>in</u> <u>Style</u> <u>and</u> <u>Poetic</u> <u>Development</u>, University of Wisconsin Studies in Language and Literature, No. 37 (Madison, 1935), p. 52.

Primary Footnotes

(The form to be used the *first* time a work is cited)

¹Paull F. Baum, <u>Ten</u> <u>Studies</u> <u>in</u> <u>the</u> <u>Poetry</u> <u>of</u> <u>Matthew</u> <u>Arnold</u> (Durham, N.C., 1958), p. 37.

    (book by a single author; p. is the abbreviation of *page*)

²René Wellek and Austin Warren, <u>Theory</u> <u>of</u> <u>Literature</u> (New York, 1949), pp. 106-7.

    (book by two authors; pp. is the abbreviation of *pages*)

³William Hickling Prescott, <u>History</u> <u>of</u> <u>the</u> <u>Reign</u> <u>of</u> <u>Philip</u> <u>the</u> <u>Second,</u> <u>King</u> <u>of</u> <u>Spain,</u> ed. John Foster Kirk (Philadelphia, 1871), II, 47.

    (an edited work of more than one volume; *ed.* is the abbreviation for "edited by"; note that whenever a volume number is cited, the abbreviation p. or pp. is *not* used in front of the page number)

⁴John Pick, ed., <u>The</u> <u>Windhover</u> (Columbus, Ohio, 1968), p. 4.

    (form for quotation from an editor's Introduction — as, for instance, in this casebook series; here *ed.* is the abbreviation for "editor")

⁵A.S.P. Woodhouse, "Nature and Grace in <u>The</u> <u>Faerie</u> <u>Queen,</u>" in <u>Elizabethan</u> <u>Poetry</u>: <u>Modern</u> <u>Essays</u> <u>in</u>

<u>Criticism</u>, ed. Paul J. Alpers (New York, 1967),
pp. 346-7.

(chapter or article from an edited collection)

[6]Morton D. Paley, "Tyger of Wrath," <u>PMLA</u>, LXXXI
(December, 1966), 544.

(an article from a periodical; note that because the volume number is cited no p. or pp. precedes the page number; the titles of periodicals are often abbreviated in footnotes but are spelled out in the Bibliography; here, for instance, *PMLA* is the abbreviation for *Publications of the Modern Language Association*)

Secondary Footnotes

(Abbreviated footnote forms to be used after a work has been cited once in full)

[7]Baum, p. 45.

(abbreviated form for work cited in footnote #1; note that the secondary footnote is indented the same number of spaces as the first line of primary footnotes)

[8]Wellek and Warren, pp. 239-40.

(abbreviated form for work cited in footnote #2)

[9]Prescott, II, 239.

(abbreviated form for work cited in footnote #3; because this is a multi-volume work, the volume number must be given in addition to the page number)

[10]<u>Ibid</u>., p. 245.

(refers to the immediately preceding footnote — that is, to page 245 in the second volume of Prescott's history; *ibid.* is the abbreviation of the Latin adverb *ibidem* meaning "in the same place"; note that this abbreviation is italicized or underlined and that it is followed by a period, because it is an abbreviation)

[11]<u>Ibid</u>., III, 103.

(refers to the immediately preceding footnote — that is, to Prescott's work again; there must be added to *ibid.* only what changes from the preceding footnote; here the volume and page changed; note that there is no p. before 103, because a volume number was cited)

[12]Baum, pp. 47-50.

(refers to the same work cited in footnote #7 and ultimately to the work cited in full in footnote #1)

[13]Paley, p. 547.
> (refers to the article cited in footnote #6)

[14]Rebecca P. Parkin, "Mythopoeic Activity in the Rape of the Lock," ELH, XXI (March, 1954), 32.
> (since this article from the *Journal of English Literary History* has not been previously cited in full, it must be given in full here)

[15]Ibid., pp. 33-4.
> (refers to Parkin's article in the immediately preceding footnote)

Bibliography Forms

Note carefully the differences in bibliography forms from footnote forms: (1) the last name of the author is given first, since bibliography items are arranged alphabetically according to the surname of the author (in the case of two or more authors of a work, only the name of the first author is reversed); (2) the first line of each bibliography item starts at the lefthand margin; subsequent lines are indented; (3) periods are used instead of commas, and parentheses do not enclose publication information; (4) the publisher is given in addition to the place of publication; (5) the first and last pages of articles and chapters are given; (6) most of the abbreviations used in footnotes are avoided in the Bibliography.

The items are arranged here alphabetically as they would appear in the Bibliography of your paper.

Baum, Paull F. Ten Studies in the Poetry of Matthew Arnold. Durham, N.C.: University of North Carolina Press, 1958.

Paley, Morton D. "Tyger of Wrath," Publications of the Modern Language Association, LXXXI (December, 1966), 540-51.

Parkin, Rebecca P. "Mythopoeic Activity in the Rape of the Lock," Journal of English Literary History, XXI (March, 1954), 30-8.

Pick, John, editor. The Windhover. Columbus, Ohio: Charles E. Merrill Publishing Company, 1968.

Prescott, William Hickling. History of the Reign of Philip the Second, King of Spain. Edited by John Foster Kirk. 3 volumes. Philadelphia: J.B. Lippincott and Company, 1871.

Wellek, René and Austin Warren. <u>Theory</u> <u>of</u> <u>Litera-</u>
    <u>ture</u>. New York: Harcourt, Brace & World, Inc.,
    1949.

Woodhouse, A.S.P. "Nature and Grace in <u>The</u> <u>Faerie</u>
    <u>Queene</u>," in <u>Elizabethan</u> <u>Poetry</u>: <u>Modern</u> <u>Essays</u> <u>in</u>
    <u>Criticism</u>. Edited by Paul J. Alpers. New York:
    Oxford University Press, 1967, pp. 345-79.

If the form for some work that you are using in your paper is not given in these samples of footnote and bibliography entries, ask your instructor for advice as to the proper form.